North Korea

North Korea

BY LIZ SONNEBORN

Enchantment of the World™
Second Series

CHILDREN'S PRESS®

An Imprint of Scholastic Inc.

New York   Toronto   London   Auckland   Sydney
Mexico City   New Delhi   Hong Kong
Danbury, Connecticut

Frontispiece: **Mass games performance**

Consultant: Charles K. Armstrong, Professor of History and Director of the Center for Korean Research, Columbia University, New York, New York

Please note: All statistics are as up-to-date as possible at the time of publication.

Book production by The Design Lab

Library of Congress Cataloging-in-Publication Data
Sonneborn, Liz.
 North Korea / by Liz Sonneborn.
 p. cm.—(Enchantment of the world. Second series)
 Includes bibliographical references and index.
 ISBN 978-0-531-23678-9 (lib. bdg.)
 1. Korea (North)—Juvenile literature. I. Title.
 DS932.S68 2014
 951.93—dc23   2013003650

1 2 3 4 5 6 7 8 9 10 R 23 22 21 20 19 18 17 16 15 14

Bicyclist in Hamhung

Contents

Left to right: **Mt. Paektu, dancers, sheep and goats, International Friendship Exhibition, Hamhung**

CHAPTER 1

The Day of the Sun

ON THE NIGHT OF APRIL 16, 2012, AN ENORMOUS crowd of people gathered at Kim Il-sung Square in Pyongyang, the capital of the People's Democratic Republic of Korea (PDRK), often called North Korea. They were there to witness a fabulous, once-in-a-lifetime spectacle. Under the stars, thousands of performers rushed into the open-air plaza and began singing and dancing in unison. The women wore *Choson-ot*, traditional loose-fitting gowns, in brilliant hues of red, yellow, and orange. Their male dance partners donned Western-style suits and ties. A chilly wind swept through the stadium as they executed their routines flawlessly. As the performance came to an end, fireworks filled the night sky.

The mass dance in Pyongyang was just one event in a weeklong celebration of the hundredth anniversary of Kim Il-sung's birth. Kim is considered the founder of North Korea, which North Koreans always call the PDRK or simply Korea. In 1948, when the country was established, he became

Opposite: **North Korea is renowned for its mass games, in which thousands of dancers and gymnasts work in unison.**

its first ruler. During his forty-six-year reign over North Korea, Kim was more than just a leader. The government promoted him as an almost godlike figure, a superhuman being whose strength, compassion, and devotion to North Korea kept the nation safe from its enemies.

A New Leader

Celebrating Kim Il-sung's birthday was nothing new to North Koreans. Referred to as the Day of the Sun, it had long been North Korea's most important national holiday. But the celebration in 2012 was special. Not only was it the one-hundredth anniversary of Kim's birth, but it was also a time of enormous change in the country.

Only a few months before, Kim's son and successor, Kim Jong Il, had died. Upon his death, North Korea suddenly had a new ruler—Kim Jong-eun, the son of Kim Jong Il and the grandson of Kim Il-sung. The great birthday festivities unexpectedly became a double celebration to honor both the legacy of Kim Il-sung and the rise to power of Kim Jong-eun.

The government of North Korea has a reputation for secrecy and hostility toward outsiders. But it issued a rare invitation to

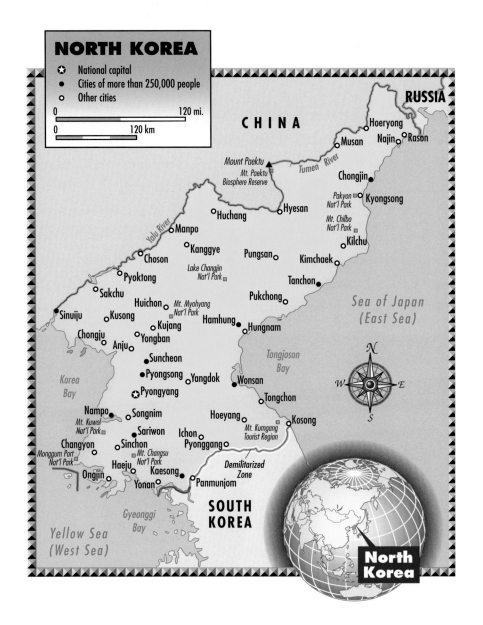

foreign journalists from around the world to come to Pyongyang and see the birthday celebration. Escorted through the country by government-assigned guides, the journalists attended a variety of events, all carefully planned to display North Korea's greatness. They saw the unveiling of a huge mosaic of Kim Jong Il's face surrounded by magnolias, the national flower.

They attended the dedication of two giant gleaming statues of the first two Kim rulers. They joined celebrations marking the completion of a new hydroelectric power plant and a three-thousand-room hotel in the center of the capital.

However, the event that made the most international news was the launching of the Unha-3 rocket. North Korea claimed the rocket would send a satellite into space, which would then broadcast songs in praise of Kim Il-sung. But the leaders of most other nations suspected it had another use.

Children sweep the steps of a giant mosaic of Kim Il-sung (right) and Kim Jong Il. Large pictures and statues of the leaders have been erected throughout North Korea.

They feared the launch was a test to find out whether North Korean engineers had developed a missile that could send nuclear weapons to other nations. If, in fact, the launch was meant to intimidate North Korea's neighbors, the show of aggression fizzled. About ninety seconds after the launch, the rocket disintegrated in midair.

A rocket lifts off from the Tongchang-ri launching site on North Korea's northwestern coast. This rocket carried a satellite into space, but some experts believe the launch site could be used to fire nuclear weapons.

An Uncertain Future

The embarrassment of the rocket launch barely put a damper on Kim's birthday celebration. Just two days later, North Korea held a massive parade as a show of its military might. In Kim Il-sung Square, thousands of uniformed soldiers marched and chanted, hailing Kim Jong-eun, who had just been given the title Supreme Leader. During the parade, more than eight hundred pieces of military hardware were on display, including a missile so large it had to be carried on a massive sixteen-wheel truck.

Shown on a giant screen, Kim Jong-eun waves to the crowd at the celebration in honor of the one hundredth birthday of his grandfather, Kim Il-sung. As the country's supreme leader, Kim Jong-eun is the head of both the government and the military.

The event took an unexpected turn when North Korea's new leader rose from his seat on a platform overlooking the square and walked to a podium outfitted with seven microphones. A young man in his late twenties, Kim Jong-eun began to read a prepared speech from a piece of paper he held in his hands. In most other countries, a leading political figure delivering a speech at a big public event would have been unremarkable. But in North Korea, it was extraordinary. During his decades-long rule, Kim Jong-eun's father had spoken to the public only once, and then said only a few words of praise for the North Korean army.

Kim spoke for twenty minutes. He delivered his speech in a calm, low tone, possibly crafted to sound like his revered grandfather. Kim talked in vague terms about his country's dire economic troubles. He even alluded to its most pressing problem—constant food shortages that leave millions malnourished. But he offered no new policies to address the nation's problems. Kim, however, was very clear on his stance on the North Korean military. He declared that, like his father, he considered the military his "first, second, and third" priorities. Kim also suggested that he had no plans to end North Korea's quest for nuclear weaponry. He told the crowd, "Yesterday, we were a weak and small country trampled upon by big powers. Today, . . . we are transformed into a proud political and military power and an independent people that no one can dare provoke."

On the anniversary of Kim Il-sung's birth, military equipment parades through Kim Il-sung Square. North Korea has a larger military than any other country in the world.

Foreign journalists reporting on Kim's speech speculated about what it might mean. His words suggested that he would follow his father's and grandfather's lead and take an aggressive stance toward foreign powers. But the fact that he appeared in public at all suggested a new leadership style and perhaps a willingness to engage with the outside world.

In this debate on North Korea's fate and future, one viewpoint was clearly absent—that of the North Korean people. The North Korean government forbids the nation's people from

North Korean children walk home from school. Children are required to attend school until age sixteen.

leaving the country or communicating in any way with the world outside North Korea's borders without government permission. One of the greatest mysteries in an extremely secretive country is what North Koreans really think of their leaders. Do they unquestionably love and revere the Kim rulers, as the government would have everyone believe? Or are they, like many outsiders, disturbed and alarmed that their government would spend US$1 billion on a birthday extravaganza while allowing many of their fellow citizens to go hungry?

North Korea has sometimes suffered devastating flooding and famine, resulting in widespread hunger.

CHAPTER 2

Mountains and Valleys

JUST AS ITS NAME SUGGESTS, NORTH KOREA IS located on the northern portion of the Korean Peninsula in northeastern Asia. A peninsula is a land formation that is nearly surrounded by water but is still connected to the mainland. To the west of North Korea is the Yellow Sea. To the east is the Sea of Japan. To North Koreans, however, these bodies of water are known by their orientation to their country. The Yellow Sea therefore is called the West Sea, while the Sea of Japan is referred to as the East Sea. The nation's lengthy coastline stretches over 1,550 miles (2,495 kilometers).

The total area of North Korea measures about 47,399 square miles (122,763 square kilometers). The country is approximately the same size as the U.S. state of Pennsylvania.

Opposite: **Visitors climb stairs at Mount Kumgang, in southeastern North Korea. The jagged mountain has been famed for its beauty since ancient times.**

Neighboring Nations

North Korea borders three other countries. To the north is the People's Republic of China, with which North Korea shares its longest border. It measures 880 miles (1,416 km). Much

North Korea's Geographic Features

Area: 47,399 square miles (122,763 sq km)

Highest Elevation: Mount Paektu, 9,003 feet (2,744 m) above sea level

Lowest Elevation: Sea of Japan, sea level

Longest Border: With China, 880 miles (1,416 km)

Shortest Border: With Russia, 11 miles (17.7 km)

Longest River: Yalu River (below), 491 miles (790 km)

Largest Lake: Heaven Lake, 3.8 square miles (9.8 sq km)

Wettest Month: July, average rainfall of 9.9 inches (25.1 cm)

Hottest Month: August, average daily high temperature of 83°F (28°C)

Coldest Month: January, average daily high temperature of 29°F (-2°C)

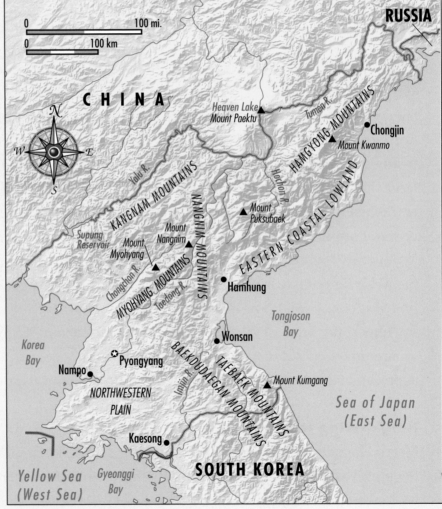

of this boundary traces the course of North Korea's two longest rivers: the Yalu and the Tumen. North Korea and China have several longstanding land disputes, including conflicting claims to several islands in these rivers. North Korea's other northern neighbor is Russia. These countries share a boundary just over 11 miles (17.7 km) in length.

The Republic of Korea, also known as South Korea, lies directly to the south of North Korea. The official border between the two halves of Korea runs through a 2.5-mile-wide (4 km) strip of land called the demilitarized zone, or DMZ. Stretching over 151 miles (243 km) of land, the DMZ was established at the end of the Korean War (1950–1953), in which North Korea and its allies fought South Korea and its allies.

North Korean soldiers peer at a South Korean soldier at Panmunjom in the Korean demilitarized zone. Panmunjom is one of only two crossing points between North and South Korea.

Along the eastern coast of North Korea, the mountains sometimes reach all the way to the sea.

Contrary to its name, the DMZ is actually not demilitarized. In fact, it is occupied by more military personnel than any other place on earth. Probably more than one million soldiers from the two Koreas are stationed along the DMZ. About twenty-eight thousand troops from the United States, an ally of South Korea, are also based there.

The Terrain

North Korea is one of the most mountainous countries in the world. About three-quarters of the land is covered with mountain ranges separated by deep and narrow valleys. North Korea's mountain ranges include the Nangnim Mountains, which run through its north-central region.

The highest mountains on the Korean Peninsula are in North Korea. Famous for its beauty, Mount Kumgang is being developed as an attraction for foreign tourists. The country's tallest peak, Mount Paektu, rises to 9,003 feet (2,744 meters) in the north along the border with China.

North Koreans are proud of the country's snow-covered mountains, which often appear in paintings and other works of art. But its largely mountainous and hilly terrain has also posed a problem throughout the nation's history. Only about 22 percent of its land is suitable for farming. Much of this farmland is found on the wide coastal plain in the west. The Taedong River and its tributaries run through this plain. This region is also the most densely populated area in the country.

With so little land available for agriculture, North Korea has often struggled to produce enough food for its population, even in years when there has been a healthy harvest. In times of drought

Jong Il Peak

One of the most celebrated sights in North Korea is Mount Paektu. The government claims that North Korean ruler Kim Jong Il was born there. In fact, he probably was born in Russia, which was then part of a nation called the Soviet Union. The North Korean government named the spot where he was said to have been born Jong Il Peak in his honor. When he died in 2011, North Korean news sources reported on several supernatural events that had supposedly occurred. One report held that the peak took on a mysterious glow with the announcement of Kim's death.

or flooding, its food production has fallen far short of its needs. In the mid-1990s, extensive flooding caused widespread famine. Although conditions have since improved, the country still relies on food aid from other nations for its people's survival.

North Korea is facing a variety of environmental challenges. One problem is loss of fertile topsoil, which has been carried away in floods. The government's efforts to establish farms along hillsides have only made this situation worse. These new farms have caused more soil erosion. Chemical fertilizers used on these farms to help crops grow also washed into nearby rivers. Because of this contamination, much of North Korea's population lacks an adequate supply of safe drinking water.

Farmhouses line a hillside in North Korea. About 40 percent of North Koreans live in rural areas.

Cities of North Korea

Traditionally, most people of the Korean Peninsula were farmers living in rural areas. But since the peninsula was divided in 1948, its population has become increasingly urban. Today, about two-thirds of North Koreans live in cities. The capital, Pyongyang, is by far the largest city in North Korea, with a population of more than three million.

Hamhung (below), North Korea's second-largest city, with a population of 768,600, is located on the country's eastern coast. Long an industrial powerhouse, it is known for its production of textiles (woven cloth and

related goods). Factories in Hamhung also produce metals, chemicals, and processed foods. The city's beaches are favorite recreational spots for residents.

To the northeast, along the Sea of Japan, lies Chongjin. It is the nation's third-largest city, home to 667,900 people. It began as a small fishing village. In the early twentieth century, Japan occupied Korea and developed Chongjin because it was close to several iron mines. Today, much of the iron and steel manufactured in North Korea comes from Chongjin.

Nampo (above) is North Korea's fourth-largest city, with a population of 366,800. The port city is located on the Taedong delta, just 30 miles (50 km) to the southwest of Pyongyang. Nampo is a center for shipbuilding and for commercial fishing. The delicious apples grown there are its best-known product.

A typhoon pounds the coast near the city of Wonsan, in southern North Korea. To be classified as a typhoon, a storm must have sustained winds of at least 74 miles (119 km) per hour.

Climate and Weather

Most of the populated areas of North Korea enjoy a relatively temperate climate. Winters are long, but there is little rain or snow. The coldest days arrive between December and March.

North Korea receives an average of about 40 inches (102 centimeters) of rain annually. Roughly 30 inches (76 cm) falls in the summer between June and September. During this period, the country sees an occasional typhoon, or tropical storm. The worst summer weather occurs in July and August, when the humidity and heat are often stifling. Although temperatures vary in different parts of the country, they generally range from highs of about 29 degrees Fahrenheit (−2 degrees Celsius) in January to about 83°F (28°C) in August.

A North Korean girl herds sheep and goats back to the stable on a snowy winter day. Snow falls in Pyongyang an average of thirty-seven days a year, and more often in mountainous areas.

Temperature extremes are particularly hard on the many North Koreans living in poverty. Few have access to air-conditioning in the summer. Even buildings in cities that are air-conditioned remain hot because of frequent power outages. In the countryside, the coldest winter nights bring even more brutal conditions. With little fuel available to heat their rustic houses, many North Koreans must brave the chilly air without any source of heat at all.

Heaven Lake

Mount Paektu, the country's highest peak, is an extinct volcano. Filling the volcano's crater is the huge Heaven Lake, one of the deepest lakes in the world. In both North Korea and neighboring China, people have claimed that the lake is home to a breed of monsters. Descriptions of these mythic monsters vary, but some accounts say they have gigantic fins or even wings.

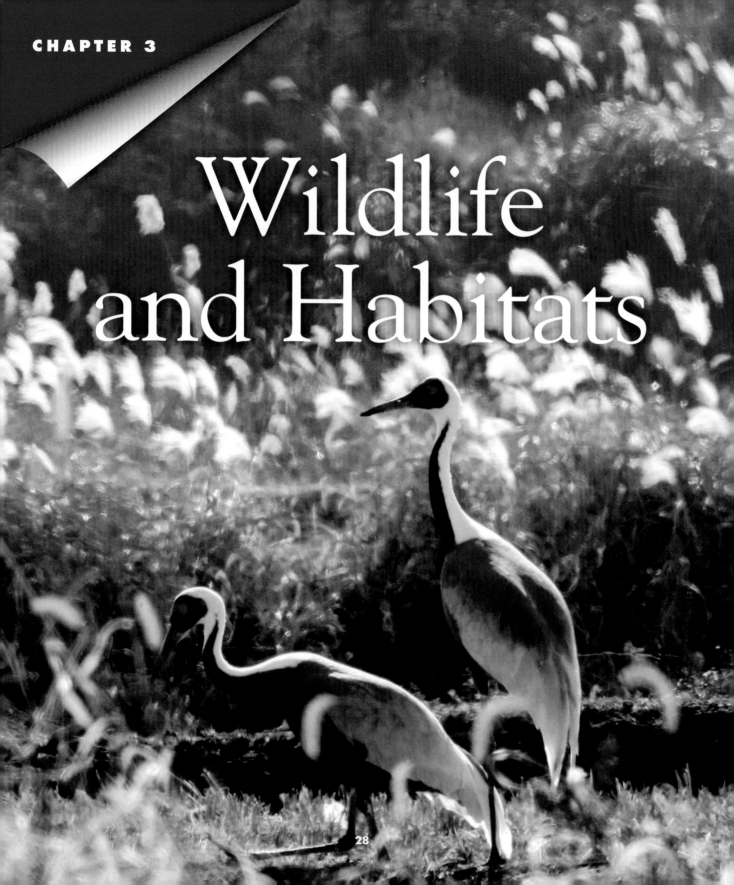

CHAPTER 3

Wildlife and Habitats

WITH LUSH FORESTS, MAJESTIC MOUNTAINS, AND fertile river valleys, North Korea has a wide variety of natural habitats. These landscapes can sustain a wealth of plants and animals. Unfortunately, in recent decades, many of these areas have been threatened by natural disasters, including typhoons and massive floods. Some habitats have disappeared as forests have been cut down to create farmland.

Opposite: **White-naped cranes are one of many bird species that spend part of the year in the Korean demilitarized zone. In the spring, they head north to breed in China, Mongolia, and Russia.**

Animals

North Korea is home to hundreds of species of animals. Small mammals, such as hedgehogs, mice, hares, rabbits, and chipmunks, live throughout the countryside. The Siberian flying squirrel and the northern pika are found in forested areas. In North Korea's wetlands, birds such as herons and cranes are common. The nation's rivers teem with eels and carp, while porpoises, dolphins, and seals live in coastal waters.

There are many other large mammals in North Korea, although their populations have shrunk with the nation's forests. These animals include foxes, lynx, wolves, deer, and

The Magnolia

The magnolia is North Korea's national flower. Blooming in early summer, magnolias are adorned with large blossoms. Their petals are bright white, while the center of the bloom is colored a brilliant red.

The magnolia plays an important role in the ancient mythology of Korea. One myth tells of a series of contests between Mireuk, the creator of humankind, and Seokga, a rival god. In one competition, they both slept near a magnolia flower. Whomever the magnolia leaned toward as they drowsed would be the winner. Although the flower grew toward Mireuk, Seokga triumphed by breaking the magnolia stem and placing the flower on his own lap. Mireuk, in a furious rage, then unleashed sorrow and evil into the world.

antelope. With their habitats threatened, some animals native to North Korea are now in danger of becoming extinct. They include the Amur leopard, the Asiatic black bear, and the Siberian tiger.

Plant Life

North Korea's best-preserved natural habitats are found in its mountainous regions in the center of the country, where few people live. There, beautiful forests of cedar, aspen, birch, and fir trees thrive as they have for centuries. Hearty Korean pines, which can grow as high as 160 feet (50 m), also flourish on mountainsides even during harsh winter weather.

The lowlands of western North Korea once sustained sizable forests. Trees native to the region include small pines, oaks, and birches. Today, however, the lowlands have largely been cleared to make way for cities and farms. Among the food plants cultivated in North Korea are soybeans, corn, potatoes, and wheat.

Diversity in the DMZ

The area of North Korea with the greatest diversity of plant and animal life is the demilitarized zone, or DMZ. This border area between North and South Korea was once full of farms, but after the Korean War, the farms were abandoned, and the zone was taken over by the military of both countries. Given that the DMZ is now filled with tanks and land mines, it may seem odd that it is also an extremely hospitable environment for wildlife. But, because the DMZ has seen no development in the last sixty years, it is one of the best-preserved natural habitats in the world.

The Chollima

North Korea's national animal, the chollima, is not actually an animal at all. It is a winged horse with its origins in Chinese mythology. The fabled chollima is said to have amazing speed. North Koreans hold that it can fly hundreds of miles a day. A great bronze statue of the chollima stands on Mansu Hill in the North Korean capital of Pyongyang.

After the Korean War (1950–1953), North Korean ruler Kim Il-sung used this beloved mythical creature to rally his people. With North Korea in ruins, his government inaugurated the Chollima Movement to rebuild the country. Kim urged his people to work at "chollima speed" to make the nation prosperous as quickly as possible.

The Kimilsungia and the Kimjongilia

According to a story told in North Korea, when Kim Il-sung visited the president of Indonesia, he admired a beautiful purple orchid in a botanical garden. After Kim asked what the flower was called, the Indonesian president declared it was the kimilsungia. Decades later, his son, Kim Jong Il, received his own floral tribute. In 1988, a Japanese botanist created a type of red begonia designed to bloom in February, the month of Kim Jong Il's birth. It was dubbed the kimjongilia (right).

Each year, the blooming of the kimilsungia and the kimjongilia are national events. A great exhibition is held in the North Korean capital of Pyongyang to show elaborate displays of the flowers. Many of the displays feature portraits of the Kims or models of historical sites. Some bouquets donated by units of the North Korean military are adorned with guns, swords, and missiles.

This accidental nature reserve features a wide variety of environments. The narrow strip of land, which stretches across the entire Korean Peninsula, includes mountains, prairies, swamps, and marshes. Isolated from the rest of the world, the DMZ supports about 2,700 species of plants and animals.

Among the most spectacular are red-crowned cranes. These rare birds, which number only about three thousand across the globe, breed along rivers in northern China and southern Russia. When the weather turns cold, they migrate south, with many spending the winter in the wetlands of the DMZ. Visitors to the DMZ often marvel at the beauty of these white-feathered cranes, whose wings span out more than 8 feet (2.4 m) as they fly.

Amur goral mountain goats are among the sixty-seven rare and endangered species found in the DMZ.

Because of the DMZ's incredible biodiversity, some environmentalists have tried to make the area into an official protected natural reserve. Some proposals have been backed by the South Korean government, but North Korea has consistently resisted these efforts.

The Pyongyang Central Zoo

In the suburbs of the capital of North Korea is the Pyongyang Central Zoo. Founded in 1959, the zoo houses some five thousand animals, including some endangered species. Although a popular local attraction, the zoo has drawn criticism for keeping its animal residents in conditions that are sometimes unsafe. It also came under fire in 2010, when Robert Mugabe, president of the African nation of Zimbabwe, ordered that pairs of zebras, giraffes, elephants, and other animals be rounded up and presented as a gift to North Korean leader Kim Jong Il. Many animal activists were outraged. They protested that the animals would not survive in the run-down North Korean national zoo.

CHAPTER 4

The Hermit Kingdom

ACCORDING TO ANCIENT KOREAN MYTHOLOGY, Hwanung, the son of heaven, went to live on Mount Paektu. There, a bear that had turned into a beautiful woman wept because she could not have a child. Hwanung took pity on the woman and married her. She soon gave birth to a son, Tangun. Tangun is still revered throughout the Korean Peninsula as the legendary founder of the first Korean kingdom.

This early state, now known as Old Choson, arose in about the fourth century BCE. It was centered on the Taedong River basin. The people of Old Choson developed sophisticated farming methods, including the use of iron plows. The presence of iron weapons at Old Choson sites suggests they also warred with other peoples.

Opposite: **Master goldsmiths lived in ancient Korea. These earrings were made about fifteen hundred years ago.**

The Three Kingdoms

The second century BCE saw the rise of the Han rulers in China, a powerful state to the north of Korea. Over the next

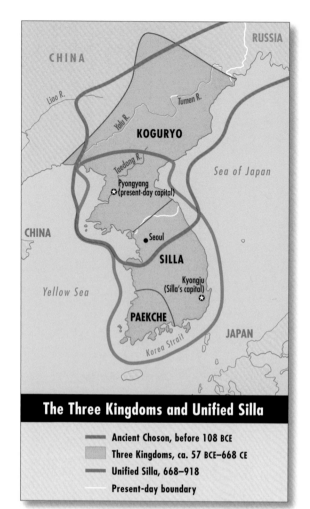

The Three Kingdoms and Unified Silla

— Ancient Choson, before 108 BCE
▨ Three Kingdoms, ca. 57 BCE–668 CE
— Unified Silla, 668–918
— Present-day boundary

few centuries, as the Old Choson civilization declined, China drew parts of Korea into its empire. In northwestern Korea, China established the colony of Nangnang, with its capital at Pyongyang.

In northern Korea, the state of Koguryo grew up along the Yalu River. In 313 CE, its leaders overthrew Nangnang and drove the Chinese there away. While Koguryo was gaining power, two states were emerging in other parts of Korea. In the south, Paekche became a major power, while in central Korea, Silla developed into the dominant force. Koguryo, Paekche, and Silla are now known to historians as the Three Kingdoms.

Silla defeated its rival states Paekche and Koguryo in 668, thereby ending the Three

The Complex of Koguryo Tombs

The Complex of Koguryo Tombs includes the only physical remains of the Koguryo kingdom. These tombs, located in North Korea and northeastern China, were probably the burial sites of kings and members of their court. The tombs themselves are made of stone, which were then covered with mounds made of stone or earth. Most interesting to historians are the many wall paintings inside the tombs. They provide valuable information about how the people of the Koguryo civilization lived, from the clothing they wore, to the food they ate, to the religious rituals they practiced.

This ceramic vase from the Silla kingdom dates to the fifth or sixth century CE.

Kingdoms period. Silla's victory marked the first time that the entire Korean Peninsula was under unified rule. Silla also soon drove off the Chinese from the peninsula's northern border. Freed from Chinese control, a unified Korea began to develop its own unique culture and society.

The period when the Silla civilization dominated was a time of peace and progress. The Silla capital of Kyongju, located in what is now South Korea near the port of Pusan, was a great center of art and learning. One of the culture's greatest achievements was the invention of woodblock printing. The Dharani Sutra, the oldest existing text printed using this technology, was created in Silla in 751.

Woodblock Printing

Woodblock printing is a method for transferring an image onto paper or cloth. The artist uses a block of wood to make the print. He or she draws a design onto the wood. The wood is then cut away around the design. This leaves only the design at the surface level of the wood. After all the wood around the design is cut away, ink is spread over the design. The woodblock is then pressed onto a piece of paper. The area that was cut away appears white. The design appears in the color of the ink.

Woodblock printing was first used in Korea in the 700s. It was not used in Europe until the 1400s.

The Koryo Dynasty

By the early tenth century, Silla was in decline. It was replaced by another powerful state, which is known as Later Koguryo. Its founder was Wang Kon, who took control in 918. He established a ruling dynasty that took the name Koryo, a shortening of the word *Koguryo*. The country name Korea comes from *Koryo*.

In power from 918 to 1392, the Koryo dynasty moved the capital from Kyongju to Kaesong in what is now southwestern North Korea. There, Buddhism became the official religion of the ruling class and other elites. The Koryo era also saw great advances in weaponry, including the use of rockets and explosives. The military grew in importance as the Koryo rulers were increasingly challenged by raids of Chinese and Japanese invaders. In 1231, Mongols from China invaded and absorbed much of the Korean Peninsula into the vast Mongol Empire.

Over time, the Mongol Empire declined, and the Koryo court became divided. One faction supported the Ming dynasty of China. The Ming supporters, led by Yi Song-gye, gained the upper hand in 1392. Yi established the Choson dynasty, which moved its capital to what is now the city of Seoul in South Korea. Especially toward the end of their rule, the Choson leaders were hesitant to deal with outsiders, a stance that earned their realm the nickname the Hermit Kingdom. This term is often used today to describe North Korea for similar reasons.

Under Choson rule, Korean society was increasingly shaped by Confucianism. This philosophy, which originated in China,

The Temple Complex of Songgyungwan, in Kaesong, was founded in the eleventh century, during the Koryo dynasty.

offered a code of personal behavior with the goal of creating a peaceful and harmonious world. It promoted respect for elder relatives and complete obedience to political authority.

More Outsiders Arrive

Korea continued to be threatened by outsiders, as Japan and China jockeyed for supremacy in eastern Asia. In the late sixteenth century, Japanese soldiers led by Toyotomi Hideyoshi invaded the peninsula and traveled north in an attempt to conquer China. Bloody battles devastated Korea during two waves of invasion in 1592 and 1597. Chinese troops intervened and saved Korea from complete ruin.

Korea was again threatened a few decades later, when the Manchu people established the Qing dynasty in China. The Qing dynasty, which ruled from 1644 to 1911, exerted considerable control over Korea during the end of the Choson era. As in the past, China also influenced Korean culture. During this time, Catholic missionaries from China arrived in hopes of spreading their religion through the Korean Peninsula.

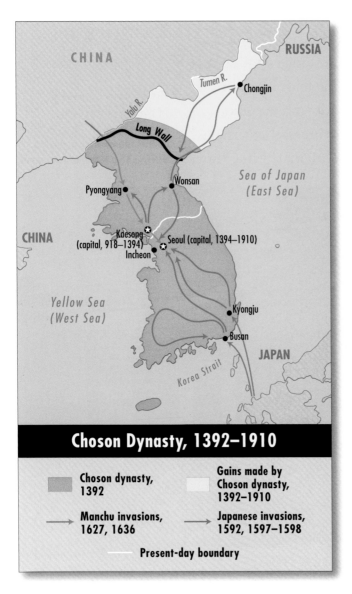

Choson Dynasty, 1392–1910

- Choson dynasty, 1392
- Gains made by Choson dynasty, 1392–1910
- → Manchu invasions, 1627, 1636
- → Japanese invasions, 1592, 1597–1598
- Present-day boundary

In both North and South Korea, Admiral Yi Sun-shin is a national hero. Born in 1545, Yi served in both the Korean army and navy. As a naval commander, he created the *kobukson*, or "turtle ship." Covered in metal plates designed to protect the soldiers inside, this vessel was the first ironclad battleship.

In 1592, the Japanese navy attacked Korea. Yi and his forces were so successful in repelling Japan's ships that he was made commander of the entire Korean navy. He lost his post after being wrongly accused of disloyalty. But in 1597, when Japan again invaded Korea, Yi was restored to his post. Once again, his fleet succeeded in protecting Korea from outside invaders. During the fighting, however, Yi was struck by cannon fire. He died in 1598.

Yi Sun-shin is considered one of the greatest naval commanders in world history. In North Korea, he is particularly revered as a symbol of the country's resistance to control by foreign powers.

Japan Takes Over

After enjoying a long period of peace, Korea was pulled into two conflicts involving foreign nations—the Sino-Japanese War (1894–1895), between China and Japan, and the Russo-Japanese War (1904–1905), between Russia and Japan. After defeating Russia, Japan emerged as the greatest power in Asia. No other nation was able to challenge Japan when it decided to take control of the Korean Peninsula. In 1905, Korea became a protectorate of Japan. Five years later, Japan turned Korea into a colony, beginning decades of Japanese occupation.

Japan set about modernizing Korea by building factories and making use of its mineral resources, most of which were found in the north. But these improvements in Korea's economy came at an enormous price. The Japanese treated the Koreans harshly. Many Koreans were pressed into slave labor. The horrors of the occupation traumatized the Korean population for decades.

A Divided Korea

During the Japanese occupation, bands of armed Koreans, largely in the north and across the border in China, waged a guerrilla war against the Japanese soldiers. But despite the Koreans' resistance, the Japanese occupation continued until 1945, when Japan was defeated in World War II (1939–1945). Japan's foes in the war included the United States and the Soviet Union, a large and powerful state that included what is now Russia. Both countries wanted to determine Korea's fate. After the Japanese were driven out of Korea, U.S. forces took control of southern Korea, while Soviet soldiers seized northern Korea. Korea was split into two parts along the 38th parallel of latitude.

The United States and the Soviet Union each wanted all of Korea to have a government modeled after its own. The United States wanted Korea to be a democratic republic, in which the people elect government officials to represent them and their needs. It also wanted the Korean economy to operate under a capitalist system, in which private owners, not the government, control trade, business, and industry.

Japanese soldiers march in Korea in the early twentieth century.

The Soviet Union wanted Korea to embrace its economic system, communism. In a communist nation, the government controls business and owns all property, distributing it to the people as the government sees fit. In theory, communism was supposed to create a fair society in which all people were treated as equals. In practice, however, large communist countries, including the Soviet Union and China, had repressive governments that allowed their people very little freedom.

On August 15, 1948, South Korea officially became the Republic of Korea. Just three weeks later, on September 9, 1948, North Korea was declared the Democratic People's Republic of Korea. Thirty-six-year old Kim Il-sung was named

Kim Il-sung meets with a Soviet military official in 1945. He became a close ally of the Soviet Union.

the premier of North Korea. Joseph Stalin, the premier of the Soviet Union, may have handpicked him. Since the Soviet takeover of the region, Korean soldiers involved in the guerrilla war against the Japanese had been favored for high-level political positions. Kim had participated in the guerrilla war, although his official biography exaggerated his involvement by claiming he had been its most important leader.

The Korean War

People in both North and South Korea considered Korea one country and did not consider the division into two to be permanent. Once in power, Kim began planning an invasion of South Korea, with

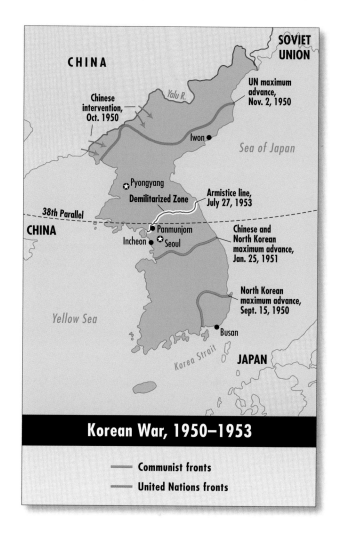

Korean War, 1950–1953

— Communist fronts
— United Nations fronts

an eye toward reunifying the Korean Peninsula. After receiving Stalin's approval, he sent his army south on June 25, 1950. The North Korean troops advanced quickly, almost reaching the southern tip of the peninsula. South Korean and United Nations (UN) forces then counterattacked. (Americans made up 88 percent of UN forces, though soldiers from twenty other nations were also involved.) By the fall, they had driven the North Koreans all the way to the Yalu River. North Korea's ally China then joined the war. Chinese troops pushed the South Korean and UN forces out of North Korea. Eventually, the two

A young child walks through rubble in Seoul, South Korea. The war left much of the Korean Peninsula in ruins.

sides reached a stalemate. Both armies were situated roughly along the border between North and South Korea.

In the summer of 1951, the two sides began negotiating an armistice—an agreement to end combat. Two more years passed until the armistice went into effect. The fighting ceased on July 27, 1953, but no formal peace treaty was ever signed to end the Korean War. Although the armistice is still in place, technically North Korea and South Korea are still at war.

The war accomplished little politically. Korea remained divided, with the north and south ruled by different governments. For the Korean people on both sides of the border, the conflict was a disaster. At least two million Koreans lost their lives, and intense bombing devastated the peninsula. North Korea saw the greatest destruction because, after the fall of 1950, most of the fighting took place in the north. After the war, with farms, factories, and buildings in ruins, the economy of North Korea was in tatters.

Taking Control

After the war, Kim Il-sung remained in power. He kept his position, in part, by having anyone who dared challenge him killed. Through such brutal means, he maintained complete control over the Korean Workers' Party, the only real political party in North Korea.

Kim also retained his leadership role because, during the next decade, his people's lives improved greatly. With the help of generous funding from the Soviet Union, he oversaw the rebuilding of North Korea and increased access to education and health care. The military also grew, employing many

In 1953, Kim Il-sung (left) signed an armistice agreement meant to ensure a peaceful solution to the Korean War.

people loyal to Kim. For North Koreans, expressing loyalty to Kim often brought great rewards, including plenty of food and the chance to live in Pyongyang, the country's capital, where living conditions were much better than in the countryside. On the other hand, anyone who criticized Kim could expect horrible treatment. Even the slightest offense might cause someone to be sent to a labor camp or even be murdered.

In addition to using harsh punishment to keep his people in line, Kim Il-sung's regime rallied North Koreans to join together to defend themselves from their supposed enemies. Under Kim, even young schoolchildren were taught to fear and hate the governments of the United States and Japan. They were told that North Korea was under constant threat of assault by these foreigners and that only Kim could keep them

Kim Il-sung's Cult of Personality

By the 1960s, paintings and sculptures of Kim Il-sung blanketed North Korea. His image appeared on billboards, public buildings, and office walls. Television and radio broadcasts, overseen by the government, constantly ran stories about Kim's feats and wisdom. Known as the Great Leader, Kim was presented almost as a god to be worshipped by all North Korean citizens. The effort to make a people passionately revere their leader is called a cult of personality. The cult built around Kim Il-sung was one of the most elaborate ever constructed. It has since been extended to include his son Kim Jong Il and grandson Kim Jong-eun, who succeeded Kim Jong Il as North Korea's all-powerful ruler.

safe. To make sure the North Korean people did not learn anything to contradict this view of the world, the government isolated the country, blocking all media from anywhere outside of North Korea.

Women work in a factory in Hamhung in 1971. Like much of the country, Hamhung had to be rebuilt after the Korean War.

Hard Times

During the 1970s, the economy of North Korea began to falter. The workforce could not keep up with unrealistic deadlines for massive building projects set by Kim's government. A lack of farmable land, too, made it difficult for North Korea to feed its population. Food shortages contradicted the government's guiding belief called Juche. *Juche* means self-reliance, or the ability to provide for all needs without the help of outsiders. Although North Korea relied heavily on funds from the Soviet Union, the government bragged about its professed independence and self-sufficiency.

Kim Il-sung was the leader of North Korea for forty-six years, until his death in 1994.

This pose became harder to maintain in the early 1990s, which marked the last years of Kim Il-sung's rule. In 1991, overwhelmed by economic troubles, the Soviet Union collapsed and dissolved into numerous smaller states. With the fall of the Soviet Union, North Korea lost much of the foreign aid it depended on. Kim made a series of overtures toward countries that North Korea had traditionally been hostile toward, including the United States and South Korea, in hopes of securing assistance from them. But just as Kim was planning a historic meeting with South Korea's president Kim Young Sam, the North Korean leader died from a massive heart attack on July 8, 1994.

Many citizens of North Korea, having been taught to think that only the Great Leader could protect them from harm, screamed and wept in the streets after learning of his death. The rest of the world watched and waited to see what would happen next. Kim had maintained complete control over the government and society of North Korea for forty-six years—longer than any other head of state in the twentieth century. In other nations, officials wondered whether the North Korean government, which maintained power largely through repression, would collapse without Kim in charge.

Kim Jong Il's Rule

Kim Jong Il did not take power until three years after his father's death. No one outside North Korea's inner circles knew the reason for the long delay. But some experts speculated that

Kim Jong Il (right) promoted a "military first" policy called *songun*. Under this policy, the military is considered the most important part of the government and society.

there was a lengthy power struggle between high officials in the military and Kim Jong Il and his supporters. Finally, Kim Jong Il was named the chairman of the Korean Workers' Party in 1997, and chairman of the National Defense Commission in 1998, making him the highest-ranking person in the government. He did not receive his father's title of president, however, because Kim Il-sung was named president for eternity, after he died.

In 1996, North Korea experienced massive flooding. It destroyed crops and damaged buildings and bridges, including this one in Haeju.

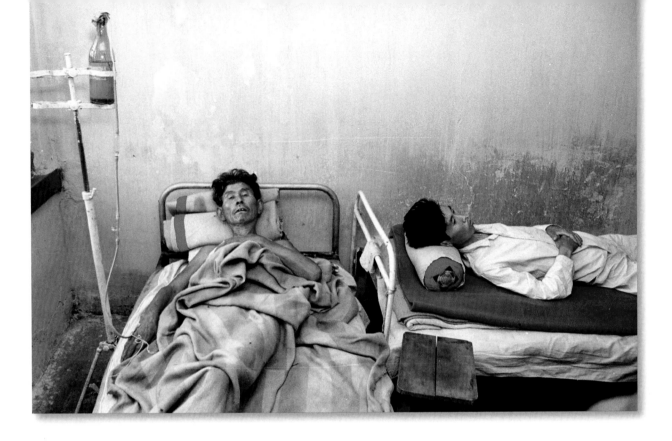

During the transition of leadership from the elder to the younger Kim, North Korea experienced terrible flooding in its prime farmlands. The resulting food shortages were an unprecedented disaster. Famine rocked North Korea, especially the countryside where millions of people had little or nothing to eat. Kim Jong Il had no choice but to request emergency supplies of food from foreign nations. In the mid-1990s, aide workers from the United Nations were allowed into the country. They were shocked by what they found. Everywhere, people were malnourished and some were starving. Estimates vary, but the massive famine may have caused the death of as many as three million North Koreans, or more than 10 percent of the population.

Any hope that Kim Jong Il's rule would be less repressive than his father's was quickly dashed. Under Kim, North Korea

North Korea suffered famine from 1994 to 1998. It is estimated that between 1 million and 3.5 million people died of starvation or hunger-related illnesses during this time.

became even more isolated from the rest of the world. He continued to send anyone considered an enemy of the state to prisons or labor camps. Some North Koreans who escaped the country talked of public executions.

To fund the lavish lifestyle of the North Korean elite, Kim Jong Il often resorted to crime. His government manufactured fake prescription drugs and counterfeited currency, or made fake bills of other countries' money. The U.S. Treasury had to redesign the $100 bill because North Korea became so skilled at counterfeiting the old design.

During Kim Jong Il's reign, North Korea also expanded its nuclear weapons program. Kim wanted to build a nuclear weapon to intimidate other nations, particularly South Korea and the United States. Additionally, with a nuclear weapon, he could argue that he was doing everything he could to keep North Korea safe from would-be invaders. Like his father, he could insist on blind obedience in exchange for protecting the North Korean people.

The United States, Japan, China, and other nations entered talks with North Korea during the first decade of the twenty-first century. They often offered North Korea food or fuel to convince the government to abandon its quest for nuclear weapons. Although they sometimes reached agreements, North Korea always broke its word or abruptly ended negotiations.

A New Leader

In late 2010, Kim Jong-eun, one of the sons of Kim Jong Il, made a rare television appearance. His father was a short

The End of the Sunshine Policy

Beginning in 1998, South Korea began making friendly overtures to its northern neighbor through its Sunshine Policy. This new approach to foreign policy sought to increase political and economic cooperation between the two countries. But, after North Korea refused to end its nuclear program, South Korean president Lee Myung-bak took a harsher line toward North Korea. His country officially abandoned the Sunshine Policy in 2010.

That year, the tensions between North and South Korea grew after two violent exchanges. In March, a torpedo sunk the *Cheonan* (left), a South Korean warship, killing forty-six sailors. The North Korean military had probably fired the torpedo, although North Korea denied all responsibility. In November, on a South Korean island, North Korean soldiers exchanged fire with South Korean troops. It was the most serious clash between the two countries since the Korean War.

In December 2012, South Korea elected a new president, Park Geun-hye. Having campaigned for the restoration of the Sunshine Policy, she is likely to try to build a better relationship with North Korea.

man who usually appeared in public wearing a tan jumpsuit and oversize glasses. Kim Jong-eun cut a much different figure. Physically larger, he wore a dark suit and high sideburns. Reports said that some North Koreans cried when they saw Kim Jong-eun, because he looked surprisingly like this grandfather Kim Il-sung. The young Kim even seemed to mimic the way his grandfather had walked and clapped his hands.

Experts on the country suggested that this was all part of a deliberate strategy to associate Kim Jong-eun with Kim Il-sung, whose rule was largely a time of prosperity in North Korea. It was certainly a signal that Kim Jong-eun would soon become

Kim Jong-eun (center, front) walks beside the hearse carrying his father's body following his father's death in December 2011.

North Korea's leader—inheriting the position from his father, as is customary. Kim Jong Il was ailing after a stroke he suffered in 2008. Although the regime tried to keep Kim Jong Il's health problems from the public, by late 2010 the regime decided it needed to prepare the Korean people for a successor.

On December 17, 2011, Kim Jong Il died suddenly of a heart attack. Two days later, it was announced that Kim Jong-eun would take his place. Just as they had after Kim Il-sung's death, world leaders watched North Korea carefully in the months that followed, wondering whether Kim Jong-eun's rise would mark a dramatic change in North Korea. They hoped that Kim Jong-eun might suspend North Korea's nuclear program and end its isolation from the rest of the world. These hopes were promptly frustrated when, in April 2012 and again in December 2012, the young Kim's government tested a missile capable of launching a nuclear weapon. Although neither launch was wholly successful, these tests sent a message: Kim Jong-eun's rule might differ in some ways from his father's, but in the short term it would not amount to a significant break from the past.

One of Kim Jong-eun's official titles is the Supreme Commander of the Korean People's Army. Here, he and other military officials observe air exercises at a North Korean air force base.

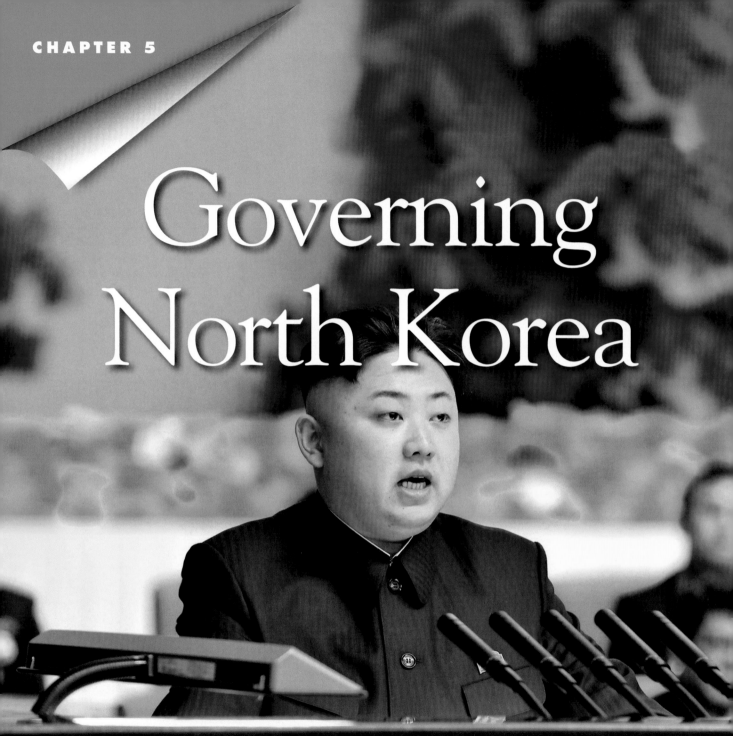

CHAPTER 5

Governing North Korea

ACCORDING TO NORTH KOREA'S CONSTITUTION, the head of government is the premier, a position held by Choe Yong-rim since 2010. The premier is assisted by three vice premiers and the twenty-eight ministers who make up the cabinet. Most of the cabinet members are appointed by the Supreme People's Assembly (SPA), North Korea's highest lawmaking body. The exception is the minister of the People's Armed Forces. The person in this post reports directly to Kim Jong-eun.

The SPA has 687 members who serve five-year terms. But the most important business conducted by the SPA is left in the hands of the Presidium, a fifteen-person group chosen from the SPA's members. The president of the Presidium is the official head of state. The Presidium can call the SPA into session, but it usually meets for only about a week once or twice a year.

Political Power

According to the constitution, the people of North Korea elect the SPA members, and all citizens age seventeen or

Opposite: **Kim Jong-eun was in his late twenties when he became the new ruler of North Korea, making him the world's youngest head of state.**

The Flag of North Korea

Adopted in 1948, the flag of North Korea has three bands, a blue band on the top and bottom and a wider red band in the middle. A slim stripe of white appears above and below the red band. On the left side of the red band is a white disc with a five-pointed red star inside.

The flag's blue bands symbolize peace, and its white stripes stand for purity. The red band and red star represent communism. The color red and stars appear prominently on the flags of other communist nations, including China and the former Soviet Union. Both of these nations were historically important allies of North Korea.

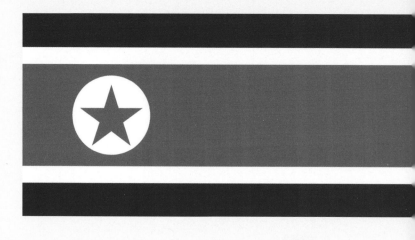

older are eligible to vote. In practice, though, North Koreans have no real say in these elections. The Korean Workers' Party (KWP), the only major political party in North Korea, handpicks the candidates. There are a few minor parties, such as the Korean Social Democratic Party and the Ch'ondoist Ch'ongu Party, but they have no real power. They only exist to allow the government to suggest that it endorses a multiparty system. Not only does the KWP choose candidates for the SPA, it generally only selects one candidate per post. Therefore, voters have no option but to vote for the single candidate on the ballot. As a result, candidates for the KWP often win elections with 100 percent of the vote.

Just as elections in North Korea are not genuine, neither is the official political structure. Neither the premier nor the president of the SPA has much influence over the government. Instead, since its founding in 1948, nearly all power in

North Korea has been held by the ruling member of the Kim family. Kim Il-sung, North Korea's first ruler, established absolute control over the country in the aftermath of the Korean War (1950–1953). He passed this position on to his son, Kim Jong Il, who in turn passed it on to his son, Kim Jong-eun. After the death of Kim Jong Il in 2011, the youngest Kim was given the unofficial title Supreme Leader, which signaled that he was following in the footsteps of his grandfather (the Great Leader) and his father (the Dear Leader). Kim has also been given the official titles of first secretary of the Korean Workers' Party, chairman of the Central Military Commission, and chairman of the National Defense Commission.

National Government of North Korea

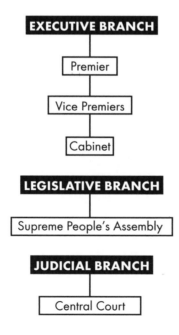

EXECUTIVE BRANCH

Premier

Vice Premiers

Cabinet

LEGISLATIVE BRANCH

Supreme People's Assembly

JUDICIAL BRANCH

Central Court

Justice and Freedom

North Korea's judicial system includes provincial and "people's" courts. But the highest judicial body is the Central Court. Its judges are appointed by the Supreme People's Assembly and are usually important members of the KWP.

Individuals have few rights under North Korea's judicial system. People accused of crimes, especially those accused of

A soldier guards a prison camp in the northeastern part of the country.

North Koreans do not have access to the full Internet. They can see only sites that have been approved by the government.

anything considered a threat or insult to the state, cannot expect a fair trial. In fact, government officials frequently have citizens rounded up and sent to prison or labor camps. People are also sometimes executed without trial.

According to North Koreans who have escaped from their country, prisoners are treated horribly. Many spend their days performing hard labor on farms or in mines. The prison living conditions are brutal and unhealthy, and prisoners are sometimes tortured. An estimated two hundred thousand North Koreans are currently being held as political prisoners.

To keep its people from questioning the regime, the North Korean government does not allow freedom of speech. If someone says anything negative about the government, he or she will likely be thrown into prison. Through its Ministry of Public Security, the government tries to monitor everything citizens say and do.

The Patriotic Song

Since 1947, North Koreans have been celebrating their country by singing "Aegukka," their national anthem. The anthem, whose name means "The Patriotic Song," is also known as "Ach'imun Pinnara," or "Let Morning Shine," which comes from its first line. With music by Kim Won Gyun and lyrics by Pak Se Yong, "Aegukka" glorifies the country's natural beauty and the rich history and culture of its people.

Let morning shine on this land of silver and gold
Three thousand li [a Chinese unit of measure] filled with natural resources.
My delightful homeland
The marvel of a wise people
With a 5,000 year-long history.
Let us commit ourselves
To taking care of Korea for all time.

Taking in the air of Mount Paektu,
Home of the soul of the working people
With strong wills, joined together with truth,
Going forward throughout the world.
A nation established by its citizens' will
Bracing waves of great strength.
Let us celebrate this Korea for all time,
Endlessly rich and strong.

There is also no freedom of the press. The North Korean press is entirely controlled by the state, and no foreign media—including newspapers, radio, or television—are allowed in the country. In this way, the North Korean people's perception of their country and the world is shaped entirely by the KWP. Through media, the party elite routinely lies to average North Korean citizens. For instance, textbooks and other official literature maintain that the Korean War began when South Korea attacked North Korea, rather than the other way around.

North Koreans read newspapers posted in a subway station in Pyongyang.

Rason lies across the Tumen River from Russia. It is an important port, often used by both Russia and China.

Regional Government

North Korea is divided into nine provinces, each with its own government. There are also two municipalities (cities) with their own provincial-level governments: the capital Pyongyang and the port Rason. All other cities are subject to their provincial governments. Two regions operate outside this administrative system—the industrial center near Kaesong and the tourist area of Kumgang. Cities and counties also have "people's committees" to make laws and "people's assemblies" to administer the local government. But all officials on both the provincial and local level are carefully monitored by the KWP, so little is done without the knowledge and consent of the elite leadership in Pyongyang.

Pyongyang

Located in western North Korea, Pyongyang is both the country's capital and, with a population of more than three million, its largest city. The city dates back to ancient times. Legend holds that it was founded in 1122 BCE. In 427 ce, it became the capital of the Koguryo kingdom.

During the Korean War, Pyongyang was completely destroyed. It was rebuilt from the ground up in the late 1950s to serve as the new capital of North Korea. Its white and gray high-rises, wide streets, and many monuments were meant to glorify the country's first leader, Kim Il-sung. Pyongyang is not as impressive as it once was. Because of North Korea's ailing economy, many of its buildings and other structures are in disrepair. But it is still the most modern city in the country, and the people who live there enjoy a much higher standard of living than most other North Koreans.

Pyongyang is North Korea's industrial and cultural center. It is home to many museums, Kim Il-sung University, and the Kumsusan Palace of the Sun, where the bodies of former rulers Kim Il-sung and Kim Jong Il can be viewed. Among the city's landmarks are the Tower of the Juche Idea and the Mansudae Grand Monument. Made of white stone and topped with a flame of red metal, the Juche Tower (below) rises 560 feet (171 m) and is brilliantly illuminated at night. The Mansudae Grand Monument features a bronze sculpture of Kim Il-sung that stands 60 feet (18 m) high. Visitors to the monument are expected to bow to the statue and lay bouquets of flowers at its feet.

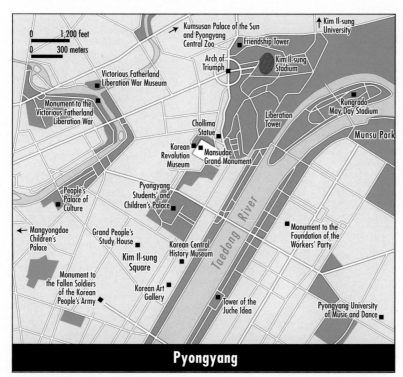

Under Military Control

Kim Jong-eun is the official leader of the vast North Korean military. Although North Korea is a communist nation, it now more closely resembles a monarchy from the Middle Ages. Like medieval kings of long ago, Kim inherited his leadership position and holds on to his authority through control over a large and powerful military force.

The Korean People's Army employs an estimated 1.2 million people, or about 4 percent of the population of North Korea. It is one of the largest standing armies in the world. All young men and some women are required to serve in the military for sometimes as long as ten years. More than seven million

About 40 percent of North Koreans are in the military or in the reserves. This is the highest percentage of any country in the world by far.

Many young people in North Korea belong to the Young Pioneers. It is like the scout movement in the United States, but emphasizes communism in addition to outdoor skills and being prepared.

additional North Koreans are in the army reserves. Many of them are in militia groups centered in small towns. These groups often carry no weapons. The reserves include millions of teenage members of the Youth Red Guard. These high school and university students meet every Saturday to perform drills to prepare them for military life.

Throughout North Korea, the country's military is celebrated. Courageous soldiers are honored in literature, art, music, and films. During Kim Jong Il's regime, the government put in place its "military first" policy. Now more than one-quarter of the country's annual income goes to the military. This allows for military personnel to receive special privileges, including better food rations and housing. Partly because of these benefits, people in uniform have a much higher social standing than North Korean civilians.

CHAPTER 6

A Struggling Economy

B

Y THE END OF THE KOREAN WAR IN 1953, BOTH North and South Korea had been battered by the bloody conflict. The two countries had to rebuild their economies practically from scratch. As South Korea struggled, North Korea bounced back with a fairly healthy economy by the 1960s and 1970s. Its growing economic strength was due in part to North Korea's possession of most of the mineral deposits on the Korean Peninsula. These natural resources helped the nation transform its economy from one based on farming to one based on manufacturing goods.

But North Korea also received a huge leg up from its powerful ally, the Soviet Union. The Soviet Union poured money into the North Korean government, which allowed it to develop different industries and invest in big building projects. But by the early 1990s, the Soviet Union was bankrupt, and its funding of North Korea came to an end. Although North Korea still received aid from other nations, most notably China, its economy never completely recovered. Later in the decade, devastating floods destroyed years of harvests, driving much

Opposite: **Workers monitor a conveyor belt at a coal mine in Pyongyang.**

The North Korean Won

The official currency of North Korea is the *won*, which is divided into one hundred *chons*. But throughout the country, people prefer to do business using U.S. dollars or Chinese *yuan*. These currencies are much more stable than the North Korean won. With rising inflation, the won is worth less and less each year. In March 2013, US$1.00 equaled 132 won, and 1 won equaled 0.89 cents.

In 2009, the country's government issued new banknotes and coins. The new currency included nine different banknotes, ranging in value from 5 to 5,000 won. Each bill is a different color, and most feature images of North Korean workers and national landmarks. The green 10-won bill, for instance, depicts soldiers from the North Korean military on the front and a Korean War monument on the back.

The government of North Korea also issues a 1-won coin as well as four coins worth a specific number of chons. The front of each coin shows the national coat of arms, while the back bears the image of a flower.

of the North Korean population into poverty and starvation. South Korea, in contrast, emerged as an economic powerhouse, attracting investors from many foreign countries and becoming one of the twenty largest economies in the world.

Working for the State

In line with communist beliefs, business enterprises and farms in North Korea are owned and run by the state. The government has strict control over all trade and banking. It also sets the prices of goods and the wages of workers. The economy of North Korea therefore operates very differently from nations under a capitalist system, such as the United States and Canada. In capitalist economies, the prices of goods are largely dictated by how much consumers are willing to pay.

Wages are not the only aspect of a worker's life that is determined by North Korea's government. The government also assigns each worker to a specific job. No one is allowed to quit and no one is free to find a different job. North Koreans are not permitted to move from one part of the country to another without special permission from the government.

Women work at a clothing factory in Kaesong, in southern North Korea. About one-quarter of North Korean workers are employed in manufacturing.

Food shortages and very low wages have driven some North Korean workers to desperation in recent years. Some have snuck across the border to take jobs in China. When they have made enough money to keep their family fed for a while, they return to North Korea. The trip is very dangerous both ways. People caught trying to leave or return to North Korea will likely lose their freedom and even sometimes their lives.

Farmworkers spread fertilizer in a rice field. North Korea produces more rice than any other crop.

Agriculture

There are about twelve million people in North Korea's labor force. Approximately four million of them work on farms. Since the late 1950s, nearly all farms in North Korea have been owned and operated by the government. These large cooperative farming operations each employ about three hundred families. Each harvest belongs to the government, which distributes the food to the public through state-run stores.

The most important food crops grown in North Korea include rice, potatoes, corn, soybeans, barley, and wheat. Farms also produce cotton and flax, which are used to make cloth, and tobacco. Workers raise livestock—especially cattle, pigs, and chickens—in areas not well suited to agriculture. Among the animal products produced in North Korea are eggs, poultry, beef, veal, goat meat, and milk. Along the coast, commercial

There are more than 2.2 million pigs in North Korea, making them one of the most common types of livestock in the nation.

What North Korea Grows, Makes, and Mines

AGRICULTURE (2010)

Rice	2,426,000 metric tons
Potatoes	1,708,000 metric tons
Corn	1,683,000 metric tons

MANUFACTURING (2009)

Cement	6,400,000 metric tons
Steel	1,300,000 metric tons
Fertilizers	466,000 metric tons

MINING

Coal (2011)	37,500,000 metric tons
Iron (2010)	1,500,000 metric tons
Phosphate rock (2010)	300,000 metric tons

fisheries supplement the country's food supply with a wide variety of fish, including mackerel, yellowtail, herring, and sardines.

Food production has improved since the 1990s, when North Korea experienced a massive famine. Yet, the country still struggles to provide enough food for its population and has to rely on aid from other countries and international organizations. The problems affecting its poor agricultural output include its small amount of good farmland; soil erosion; and a lack of fertilizer, tractors, and other modern farm equipment. Poor management on the farm collectives has also prevented North Korea from making the most of its limited agricultural resources.

Manufacturing and Energy

About two-thirds of North Korean laborers work in the manufacturing and service sectors. Goods made in North Korea include machines, textiles, weapons, and processed foods, such as canned fish. Fairly rich in mineral resources, the country also produces coal, iron ore, magnetite, limestone, copper, lead, and zinc. North Korea exports products from its factories and mines to other nations, such as China, Russia, Thailand, and South Korea.

Overall, however, North Korea's industrial production is stagnant. In recent decades, its government has spent so much money on the military that it has little left to invest in its factories. Much of its manufacturing machinery is old and not well maintained. As a result, North Korea has to import many more goods than it can export to its trading partners.

One of the nation's most important imports is oil. North Korea has very limited oil deposits so it has to buy from other countries just about all the oil and gasoline it uses. Oil shortages are common. Particularly in the countryside, people usually have to use wood for fuel, which has contributed to the loss of forestland. With forests diminishing, there is less

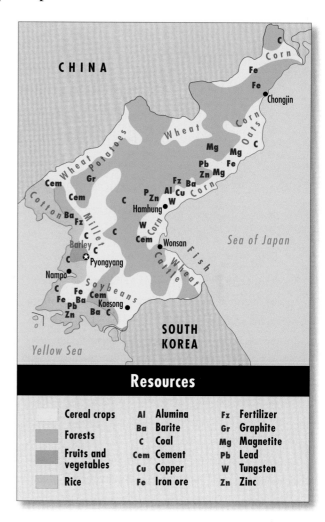

Resources

Cereal crops	Al	Alumina	Fz	Fertilizer
Forests	Ba	Barite	Gr	Graphite
	C	Coal	Mg	Magnetite
Fruits and vegetables	Cem	Cement	Pb	Lead
	Cu	Copper	W	Tungsten
Rice	Fe	Iron ore	Zn	Zinc

wood available for construction. Deforestation also leads to soil erosion, which in turn destroys much-needed farmland.

Attracting Investors

Unlike its neighbor to the south, North Korea has had trouble attracting foreign investors. The government's constantly changing foreign policy and controversial nuclear weapons program has made most investors afraid that the country and its relationship with the rest of the world is dangerously unstable.

Still, since 2002, North Korea has made some modest economic progress by creating the Kaesong Industrial Region in cooperation with South Korea. The Kaesong Industrial Region is located in southern North Korea close to the demilitarized zone. At the industrial park there, North Koreans work for low wages at about one hundred factories owned by South Korean companies.

The Mount Kumgang Tourist Region

Because of its hostility toward outsiders, the North Korean government has forbidden most tourists from visiting the country. But in 2002, it worked with a South Korean company to establish the Mount Kumgang Tourist Region to accommodate vacationers from South Korea. The area offered foreign tourists beautiful mountain scenery and excellent skiing.

In July 2008, a South Korean woman visiting the area was shot and killed by North Korean troops. The two countries issued contradictory reports about the incident. Although the facts are still murky, the shooting ended most of the tourist traffic across the border.

To increase trade with China and Russia, North Korea has been developing the northern port towns of Rajin and Sonbong, which are now known by the name Rason. Recently, the government has also worked to establish the Sinuiju Special Administrative Region along the border with China. It is a little like a laboratory, through which North Korea can experiment with running businesses modeled more on a capitalist economic system.

A woman sells fruits and vegetables at a private market. Private markets first appeared in North Korea in the mid-1990s.

Making Reforms

In the past, North Koreans could buy goods only at state-run stores. Recently, however, North Korea has experimented with the introduction of private markets. At private markets,

A North Korean waitress serves food at a hotel in Jiangyin, China. An increasing number of North Koreans are allowed to work outside the country, especially in China.

individual vendors can sell local food and other goods. Items often include imported products, such as electronics from China. The private markets have proved very popular because they are usually better stocked than state stores. In 2010, North Korea considered closing the markets. Some shoppers were so upset that they attacked security officers sent to patrol the markets. This rare act of civil unrest demonstrated just how important the markets have become to average citizens.

Reports suggest that North Korea may be experimenting with giving workers on farms and in factories more independence. It is said that some farmers are allowed to keep up to one-third of the food they grow to sell at private markets. This measure is meant to encourage farmers to increase their over-all harvests. Reports indicate that at a few factories, workers are being given more say in how they run their businesses. For instance, they might be permitted to decide what they should manufacture based on what consumers want and to choose how best to sell and market their goods.

Many of these economic reforms have been encouraged by China, which now provides the largest amount of aid that North Korea receives. China recognizes that the more North Korea's economy grows, the less Chinese aid it will need. One of North Korea's boldest new economic experiments is to allow some laborers to cross the border to work in Chinese factories. Instead of punishing or imprisoning North Koreans who want to work in China, the government charges them a fee for this right. The guest worker program helps North Koreans find better paying jobs and adds to the national treasury. But for North Korea, it represents a big change and a big risk. By exposing even a few citizens to the world outside, the government may not be able to control what new ideas and knowledge people may share when they come home.

The Metric System

North Korea uses the metric system as its official system of weights and measures.

Metric measures of distance

1 centimeter = 0.39 inches
1 meter = 3.28 feet
1 kilometer = 0.62 miles

Metric measures of volume

1 liter = 1.06 quarts

Metric measures of weight

1 kilogram = 2.20 pounds

A Revalued Currency

In late 2009, the government of North Korea announced that it was issuing a new won, the national currency. The people of North Korea were given only a few days to exchange their old currency for the new one. In addition, they were allowed to exchange only a limited amount of their old bills and coins. The move was probably meant to destroy the businesses of traders on the black market—people who buy and sell goods without the permission of the government—by wiping out their stores of cash. But average North Koreans were also hurt by these restrictions. They lost almost all of whatever meager savings they had been able to put away.

CHAPTER 7

The North Korean People

WITH MORE THAN TWENTY-FOUR MILLION PEOPLE, North Korea is the forty-ninth most populous country in the world. Although it covers more area than South Korea, North Korea's population is just about half that of its southern neighbor.

Overall, North Korea has a relatively young population. About 22 percent of North Koreans are under the age of fifteen. Only 9 percent are older than sixty-four. In contrast, 13.5 percent of Americans are over the age of sixty-four.

North Korea has almost no ethnic diversity. Since its beginnings, North Korea has been closed to outsiders. As a result, it has almost no immigrants living within its borders. There are a few very small communities of Chinese and Japanese residents. In addition, North Korea is home to a tiny number of foreign diplomats who represent their countries in dealings with the North Korean government. Otherwise, the vast majority of people in the country are of Korean ancestry.

Opposite: **Children go roller-skating in a square in Pyongyang. The average North Korean family has two children.**

Population of the Largest Cities (2008 est.)

Pyongyang	3,255,300
Hamhung	768,600
Chongjin	667,900
Nampo	366,800
Wonsan	363,127

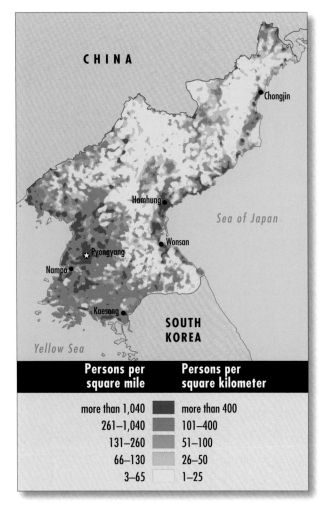

CHINA

Chongjin

Hamhung

Sea of Japan

Wonsan

Pyongyang

Nampo

Kaesong

SOUTH
KOREA

Yellow Sea

Persons per square mile		Persons per square kilometer
more than 1,040		more than 400
261–1,040		101–400
131–260		51–100
66–130		26–50
3–65		1–25

Ethnic Groups

Korean	more than 99%
Chinese, Japanese, or other	less than 1%

Measuring Loyalty

Although most North Koreans have the same ethnic background, there are still some deep divisions in North Korean society. However, these divisions have their origins in politics rather than in race or ethnicity. The people of North Korea are divided into three social classes determined by their relationship to the government—the loyal, the hostile, and those in the middle, who are wavering in their support.

People deemed loyal to the government are held in the highest esteem. They are given the best jobs, housing, and other benefits. Loyal North Koreans make up most of the population of the capital Pyongyang, where people have a much higher standard of living than elsewhere in the country. At the very top of the loyal class are the officials close to the Kim rulers. Although their lives are shrouded in secrecy, many rumors suggest that they enjoy a luxurious existence other North Koreans could scarcely imagine.

People of the neutral class struggle to survive day-to-day. Although they are monitored by the authorities for signs of disloyalty, they generally are not persecuted by the government. Those deemed hostile, on the other hand, suffer enormously because of their supposed crimes against the state. They are sent to prisons or labor camps, often for the smallest offenses.

Escaping North Korea

North Korea prohibits its citizens from leaving the country without permission, but in desperation, thousands of North Koreans try to escape every year. Most cross the border into China, either with the hope of staying in that country or of working for a time and returning home to their families.

Between 2002 and 2012, an estimated twenty-three thousand North Koreans, mostly young adults, managed to make their way into South Korea. For most, the journey was long and difficult. One young woman explained to a reporter from the

Passengers emerge from the subway in Pyongyang, the only North Korean city with a subway system.

In 2012, the Chinese arrested some North Koreans who were trying to escape through China. People in Seoul, South Korea, protested, asking China not to force the North Koreans to return home, for fear they would be killed.

British Broadcasting Corporation (BBC) that she fled North Korea after she was caught listening to pop music from South Korea, a crime that would likely land her in a labor camp.

Those people who escape to South Korea are often overwhelmed by their new country. The North Korean refugees share a language and similar cultural background with South Koreans. But life in prosperous South Korea is so different from what the North Koreans are used to that they feel disoriented. As one young refugee explained, "I felt like someone from the 1970s who was put on a time machine and dropped in the twenty-first century."

North Korean escapees are particularly shocked that South Korea is nothing like what they have been led to believe. In North Korea, authorities told them that people in South Korea are starving and miserable. Many refugees are therefore stunned by the sight of South Korean grocery stores stocked with every imaginable type of food. Others are dismayed by how little their North Korean education has prepared them for the outside world. Much of their schooling was devoted to stories of the greatness of North Korea's leaders, leaving them with poor preparation in their fields of study.

North Korean refugees have also suffered from discrimination in South Korea. South Koreans often look down on North Koreans, mocking their accents and lack of education. The South Korean government has instituted programs to help North Koreans adjust to their new society, offering them classes about life in South Korea and giving them free housing and tuition to top universities. But the transition remains difficult. One young refugee, plagued by nightmares about his experiences in North Korea, dropped out of school and spent a full year never leaving his apartment. Coaxed into returning to college, he said, "I must succeed this time. But whatever I do here, I still always ask myself, 'What am I? Where do I belong?'"

Korean Words and Phrases

Ne	Yes
Aniyo	No
Annyong haseyo	Hello/How are you?
Annyonghi kyeseyo	Good-bye
Shille hamnida	Excuse me
Komapsumnida	Thank you
Ch'on manyeo	You're welcome
Chuseyo	Please
Ch'oesong hamnida	Sorry

라남의 로동계급처럼 모든것을 자체의 힘과 기술로 !

Traditionally, Korean was written in columns from top to bottom. Now, it is usually written in rows left to right.

The Korean Language

Despite their many differences, North Koreans and South Koreans do have one thing in common—their language. About seventy million people around the world are fluent in Korean. Most live on the Korean Peninsula. But there are also sizable numbers of Korean speakers in other nations, including China, Japan, and the United States.

In various regions of the Korean Peninsula, people speak slightly different dialects, or versions, of the Korean language. Nevertheless, nearly all speakers of Korean can understand each other. In North Korea, the favored version of Korean is the dialect spoken in Pyongyang.

Throughout history, the Korean language absorbed words from other languages, especially Chinese, Japanese, and English. To keep the Korean language pure, the government of North Korea has actively discouraged the use of foreign words. However, many still creep into everyday speech. For instance, it is not unusual to hear North Koreans talking about "cameras" or "television."

Not many North Koreans know a second language. Elderly people, however, are likely to know some Japanese, which they were taught in school during the period when Japan occupied the Korean Peninsula. The most common language taught in North Korean schools used to be Russian, but increasingly students are taught to speak English. It is probably the second most common language heard on the Korean Peninsula.

Since its founding, North Korea has encouraged national pride by promoting knowledge of Korean. As a result, the country has a literacy rate among adults of about 99 percent.

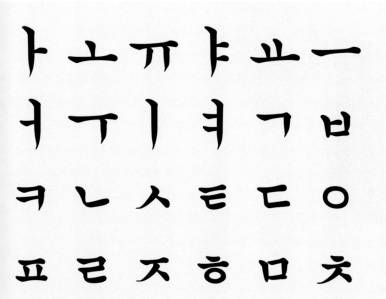

The Choson Muncha Writing System

In the 1400s, King Sejong of the Choson dynasty gathered a team of scholars. He wanted them to develop a system for writing the Korean language that did not rely on Chinese characters. The result was a writing system that is called Choson muncha in North Korea and Hangul in South Korea. Choson muncha uses twenty-four symbols. It is said to be very easy to learn. Someone can learn to write the Korean language in just a few hours, although it takes longer to truly master it.

CHAPTER 8

A Faithless State

ACCORDING TO THE CONSTITUTION OF NORTH Korea, its citizens are guaranteed freedom of religion. However, the government has long condemned religion as inconsistent with the ideals of communism. Since the 1950s, it has all but banned any religious activity. Some people, especially Christians, have been persecuted for their religious beliefs. As a result, few North Koreans express religious views or openly practice any religion.

Opposite: **A female shaman stands before a table filled with gifts to the gods in an image from an old Korean book on shamanism.**

Korean Religious Traditions

Several religious traditions have played an important role in North Korea's history. The oldest religious tradition on the Korean Peninsula is shamanism. Shamanism was not organized around a single god or authority. It instead focused on religious figures called shamans, who claimed to be able to communicate with the spirit world and the dead. Believers would call on shamans, who were often women, to ask for help from spirits and deceased relatives.

Religion in North Korea

Ch'ondogyo
　　　2.7 million people

Buddhism
　　　10,000 people

Protestantism
　　　10,000 people

Roman Catholicism
　　　4,000 people

A Buddhist monk prays at a temple in Kaesong.

In about 370 CE, the Chinese introduced Buddhism into Korea. This religion, which originated in India, was based on the teachings of a holy man called Buddha. He believed that people could relieve their suffering and achieve inner peace by letting go of all desire. Buddhism also held that after people died, they were born again, entering a cycle of death and rebirth that never ended. The quality of each life was determined by the person's karma, all the good or bad deeds that person had done in the past.

Buddhism grew in importance during the Koryo period. It became popular with both average Koreans and Korean royalty. Some members of the royal family even became Buddhist monks. These monks gave up the comforts of the court to live in monasteries, religious communities where they spent their days studying and practicing Buddhist beliefs.

Under the Choson dynasty, Buddhism lost favor with the Korean kings. They forced Buddhist monasteries out of cities and into the countryside. At the same time they rejected Buddhism, they embraced another belief system—Confucianism.

Confucius was a Chinese scholar who lived in the sixth century BCE. He instructed his students about ways they should behave in order to live a good and orderly life. According to his teachings, people should be decent, honest, and kind to one another. They should love their families and pay proper respect to their elder relatives and ancestors. Confucius also believed that citizens had an obligation to obey their rulers, an idea that the Korean kings found appealing.

Confucius was born in what is now Shandong Province on the central coast of China. He became a teacher, the first in China known to support the idea that education should be widely available.

Because it offers instructions on how best to live, Confucianism is often called a philosophy. But there are some aspects to it that make Confucianism seem more like a religion. For instance, believers often perform elaborate rituals to honor their dead relatives.

Protestant missionaries began traveling to Korea in the 1800s.

Spreading Christianity

During the 18th century, a group of Korean officials visited China. There, they met some priests who had come to China to convert people to Roman Catholicism, one form of Christianity. The officials invited the priests to establish a Catholic church in their homeland. About one hundred years later, Christians from Protestant denominations came to Korea to spread their religion. They included Presbyterians, Methodists, and Episcopalians. By the early twentieth century, the city of Pyongyang was home to many churches of a variety of denominations, making it the leading center for Christianity on the Korean Peninsula. By some accounts, the mother of North Korea's first ruler, Kim Il-sung, was a Christian.

During the Japanese occupation of Korea in the early twentieth century, Christians were persecuted, but Pyongyang remained the home of a sizable Christian community. After the establishment of North Korea, government hostility

Catholics attend a service in Pyongyang. The city once had a large Christian population, but many Christians fled to South Korea when Korea was divided.

toward Christians increased. Many Korean Christians in the north fled to South Korea during the chaos of the Korean War. In the war years, most of North Korea's houses of worship—including Christian churches and Buddhist temples—were destroyed. Today, the number of openly practicing Christians in North Korea is small, although there may be more Christians who worship secretly.

Ch'ondogyo

Most of Korea's religious traditions—including Buddhism and Christianity—originated in other places. But a religion called Ch'ondogyo (meaning "religion of the heavenly way") originated on the Korean Peninsula.

First called Tonghak (Eastern learning), Ch'ondogyo was founded by Ch'oe Che-u in 1860. He was upset by the growing influence of Western nations such as Great Britain and France in the affairs of Asian countries. Combining elements of Buddhism, Confucianism, and Roman Catholicism, his new religion taught that humans and God were one and sought to bring peace to the world. He believed that by adopting this religion the Korean people would be strong enough to resist foreign influences.

Ch'ondogyo developed a large following throughout Korea, particularly among poor farmers. It inspired some to rebel against their government, which led to Ch'oe's arrest and execution. However, his religion lived on. According to some estimates, 2.7 million people in North Korea belong to this religion. There is a Ch'ondogyo-based political party in North Korea, but it has no real power.

Founder of the Unification Church

Sun Myung Moon was the founder of the international Unification Church, which combined Christian beliefs with elements of Confucianism and other religious traditions. He was born in 1920 in what is now northwestern North Korea. He said that when he was about fifteen, he had a vision of Jesus that inspired him to begin preaching. In 1946, he was accused of spying for South Korea and thrown in prison. He escaped to South Korea during the Korean War and began attracting followers to his new religion.

Moon's Unification Church grew quickly in Korea and Japan. He moved to the United States in 1972, where he gradually found more converts, especially among young people. Critics declared that Moon's movement was less a legitimate religion than a cult. The mass weddings (above) he performed were one element that led to this criticism. Also, critics accused Moon of manipulating his followers by depriving them of sleep and food and subjecting them to other techniques of mind control.

In the 1980s, Moon was found guilty of tax evasion and spent time in prison. Once released, he continued his work as the head of the Unification Church, which has sent missionaries to nearly two hundred countries. In 2012, Moon died at the age of ninety-two.

The Pohyon Buddhist temple sits on Mount Myohyang in the central part of the country. The temple was founded a thousand years ago.

Changing Views

The North Korean government continues to discourage all formal religious observances. But in recent decades, it has loosened some of its religious restrictions. For instance, in 1992, it declared that some buildings could be constructed for religious uses. Some experts, however, do not think that the government is genuinely embracing greater religious freedom. They suggest these measures are little more than a show to make outsiders think the regime has grown more tolerant of religion.

There are now about three hundred Buddhist temples in North Korea. The government has preserved several important temples as historical monuments. In Pyongyang, there are four churches—one for Roman Catholics, two for Protestants, and one for members of the Russian Orthodox faith. North Koreans are also now permitted to take courses in religious studies at Kim Il-sung University, the country's most prestigious university.

Religious observance plays little role in most North Koreans' lives. In some ways, however, their religious traditions still influence their behavior and values. Confucianism has been especially important in shaping North Korean society. Particularly significant is Confucianism's tenets that elders must be respected and rulers must be obeyed.

Honoring Ancestors

One of the legacies of Confucianism in North Korea is the practice of ancestor worship as seen in the annual Chusok celebration. Chusok is a festival during which people give thanks for the fall harvest. Traditionally, during Chusok people traveled to the homeland of their ancestors and cleaned their dead relatives' graves. In North Korea, where people are not allowed to move freely without government permission, such a trip is often impossible. Instead, family members might gather for a picnic, sometimes carrying in tow an urn with the ashes of a revered dead relative. People in South Korea who are originally from North Korea bow in the direction of the north during the ritual (left).

CHAPTER 9

Art and Culture

As with every other aspect of life in North Korea, all types of art—from sculpture and painting to music and dance to film and television—are influenced by the state. Artists are not permitted to use their work to express their own view of the world. Instead, all public art in North Korea has a single goal—to glorify the leaders of the Kim dynasty and its regimes.

Glorifying the Ruler

Any visitor to North Korea is struck by one extraordinary thing: images of the Kim rulers, in particular Kim Il-sung, are everywhere. Statues, posters, and murals of Kim Il-sung, his son, and his grandson adorn almost every public space. Even people's clothing bears the image of the Great Leader. Since the 1970s, North Koreans have been required to wear a badge with a portrait of Kim Il-sung to show their loyalty to the government. People traditionally place the badges on the left side of their garments, possibly to keep them close to the heart. Recent reports suggest that since Kim Jong Il's death, badges with dual portraits of Kim Il-sung and his son are becoming more popular.

The government only allows the artists it most trusts to create images of the Kim leaders. Officials tell the artists exactly what to paint and how to paint it. As a result, the images they produce depict their subjects in a very specific style, leaving little room for personal artistic flourishes. The way official artists portray the Kim rulers is meant to send a message. Kim Il-sung is often shown smiling and bathed in sunshine against a blue sky. These sunny portraits are meant to remind North Koreans that during his reign the country was relatively prosperous. On the other hand, Kim Jong Il more frequently appears against a backdrop of violent waves hitting the seashore. These images suggest that only Kim Jong Il had the power to protect the North Korean people from foreign powers.

The International Friendship Exhibition

The Korean government funds many museums to glorify the rule of Kim Il-sung, including the International Friendship Exhibition. The complex is located on Mount Myohyang, a resort area known for its beautiful waterfalls and fields of summer flowers. The largest part of the International Friendship Exhibition is a series of 130 rooms filled with about one hundred thousand gifts that were given to Kim Il-sung. On display are many presents from world leaders, including a train car from Chinese chairman Mao Zedong and a limousine from Soviet president Joseph Stalin.

North Korean Literature

Writing is tightly controlled by the North Korean government. Authors approved by the regime belong to the Choson Writers' Alliance. They are the only writers allowed to publish their works in North Korea.

Like visual artists, writers are expected to use their talents to celebrate the Kim dynasty. Many stories about Kim Il-sung follow the same pattern. An aide to Kim tells him there is a problem at a factory or farming collective. After they travel there together, Kim announces a solution and the aide is amazed at Kim's great vision and wisdom. In these stories, Kim Il-sung also often expresses sympathy for a common person who is cold, tired, or hungry. Other characters then begin to weep, moved by the Great Leader's love of his people. Stories about both Kim Il-sung and Kim Jong Il emphasize how long and hard they worked for the good of North Korea. These tales are meant to encourage average citizens to work hard on behalf of their leaders.

Books by and about North Korea's leaders line the shelves in the country's bookstores.

A Beloved Poet

One of the most famous women in Korean history, Hwang Jin Yi, was born in about 1506. She was a *kisaeng* in the court of Jungjong, a king of the Choson dynasty. Kisaeng were young women charged with amusing and entertaining people of high rank. Known for her intelligence and beauty, Hwang was an accomplished poet. A few of her works, written in a traditional Korean form called *sijo*, have survived. Her favorite subjects included the majesty of the Korean landscape and the sorrow of lost love. In 2002, North Korean novelist Hong Sok-chung published *Hwang Jin-i*, a historical novel about her life. Hwang has also been the subject of a recent film and television series in South Korea.

In addition to being the subjects of much modern North Korean literature, Kim Il-sung and Kim Jong Il are also said to have written hundreds of books themselves. In fact, most of the books available in North Korea's bookstores were supposedly written by the Kim leaders. Their works are also prominent in the collection of the Grand People's Study House, the largest library in North Korea. Located in Pyongyang, it houses millions of volumes, which can be delivered to readers' tables on a conveyor belt system.

The Performing Arts

The Korean government is an enthusiastic sponsor of the performing arts. Many talented performers study at the Pyongyang University of Music and Dance. Students learn about Western art forms, such as ballet and orchestral music, as well as traditional Korean court music and folk songs and dances.

North Korea is particularly proud of its State Symphony Orchestra. The orchestra has performed in various countries, including Japan, Poland, and South Korea. In 2012, a planned visit to the United States was put on hold after a North Korean missile launch increased tensions between the two countries. Four years earlier, however, in a rare cultural exchange, the New York Philharmonic, a premier American orchestra, performed in Pyongyang.

The most lavish theatrical productions in North Korea are operas. As state-endorsed entertainments, many celebrate the achievements of North Korea under communist rule. For instance, one recent opera told the story of the construction of a hydroelectric dam. Among the most famous North Korean operas is *The Flower Girl*, which Kim Il-sung supposedly wrote when he was a young man. It is a tale of a poor rural girl in the 1930s,

Western classical music is popular in North Korea. In 2012, North Korea's Unhasu Orchestra traveled to Paris to play with the Radio France Philharmonic Orchestra.

when North Korean guerrilla forces were battling the Japanese occupying their country. The opera was made into a very popular film in 1972. Hong Yong-hee, the actress who played the title role, is pictured on the North Korean one-won banknote.

Film in North Korea

Under the rule of Kim Jong Il, the government of North Korea provided lavish funding to its film industry. A great film lover, Kim was an enthusiastic supporter of Pyongyang Film

The New York Philharmonic played in Pyongyang in 2008. It was the country's first significant cultural event by an American group since the end of the Korean War.

Studios. The studio features several film sets, including ones that depict an ancient Korean town, a South Korean street, and a Japanese setting. North Korea has claimed that the studio produces dozens of movies a year, but the actual number is probably far less. The North Korean government also sponsors the Pyongyang International Film Festival, which is held every other year in September.

Various reports suggest that Kim Jong Il was a great fan of Hollywood movies. But the government has given its approval for only three American films to be screened in North Korea—*The Sound of Music* (1965), *Home Alone* (1990), and *Titanic* (1997). Typical North Korean-made movies include *Love, Love, My Love* (1985), which tells the story of Chunhyang, a popular character in Korean folk stories. Another favorite is *Pulgasari* (1985), a monster movie similar to the Japanese classic *Godzilla*.

The Schoolgirl's Diary concerns a teenager's efforts to understand her parents and the needs of society. It became the first North Korean film released in the West when it was shown in France in 2007.

Choi Eun-hee (left) and Shin Sang-ok (right) were forced to spend eight years in North Korea before escaping in 1986.

Both *Love, Love, My Love* and *Pulgasari* were made by Shin Sang-ok, a noted South Korean director. Kim Jong Il was appalled by the quality of North Korean films, so he ordered intelligence officials to kidnap Shin and his wife, film star Choi Eun-hee, and bring them to North Korea. Shin has said that during this bizarre episode he was forced to make films under Kim's watchful eye. When Shin and Choi were caught trying to escape, Kim sent them to a prison camp, from which they were released after four years. Shin produced seven films for Kim Jong Il before he and Choi finally escaped from North Korea while attending a film festival in Vienna, Austria.

Playing Sports

Like people everywhere, North Koreans enjoy playing and watching a wide variety of sports. In parks and open areas, people come together for impromptu games of volleyball. The game is one of few that is socially acceptable for men and women to play together. Martial arts, particularly tae kwon do, and gymnastics are popular, too, especially with children. In Pyongyang, the social elite can go bowling or play golf. The Pyongyang Golf Complex, the only golf course in the country, now hosts the annual Democratic People's Republic of Korea (DPRK) Amateur Golf Open, which attracts golfers from around the world.

North Korean tae kwon do players demonstrate their skill. Tae kwon do, which was developed in Korea, features many high kicks and jumps.

The North Korea national soccer team qualified for the World Cup, the world's most prestigious soccer tournament, in 2010.

North Korea boasts a national hockey team, which belongs to the International Ice Hockey Federation. But the most important spectator sport in North Korea is soccer. Teams from the country's men's and women's soccer leagues battle one another in Kim Il-sung Stadium. North Korea also has a national team, which first competed in the international World Cup in 1966. The team is named the Chollima, after a mythological winged horse that can travel at great speed.

Pak Song-chol carried the North Korean flag during the opening ceremonies of the 2012 Olympics. He competed in the marathon, a long-distance running event that travels over 26 miles (42 km).

Since 1972, North Korea has sent athletes to many summer and winter Olympic Games. They have won medals in several sports, including boxing, wrestling, judo, and speed skating. In 2012, fifty-six North Koreans participated in the Summer Games and won four gold medals (three in wrestling and one in judo) and two bronze medals (one in wrestling and one in weight lifting). Although North Korea rarely

allows the broadcasting of any foreign news, the government agreed to show five hours of daily Olympic coverage so North Koreans could celebrate their athletes' victories.

The most spectacular athletic event held in North Korea is the annual Arirang Mass Games. During most of August and September, thousands of North Koreans gather nightly for the games at the Rungrado May Day Stadium in Pyongyang. With some 150,000 seats, it is thought to be the biggest stadium in the world.

During the games, athletes display their martial arts and gymnastic skills. They are joined by dancers performing in unison and wearing spectacularly colored costumes. But the most fantastic part of the extravaganza is the tens of thousands of children holding books of cards they can flip back and forth. These children hold up the colorful cards and, by flipping them all at the same time, create a series of enormous pictures. These depict beautiful natural scenes, the faces of the Kim leaders, and political slogans. Flipping the cards at just the right time is no easy feat. Like all the performers in the Arirang, the children have to practice for months each year to make sure they perform their part correctly.

Thousands of people hold up cards to make a huge picture that reads, "Eternal Sun, Arirang" at the Arirang Mass Games in 2008.

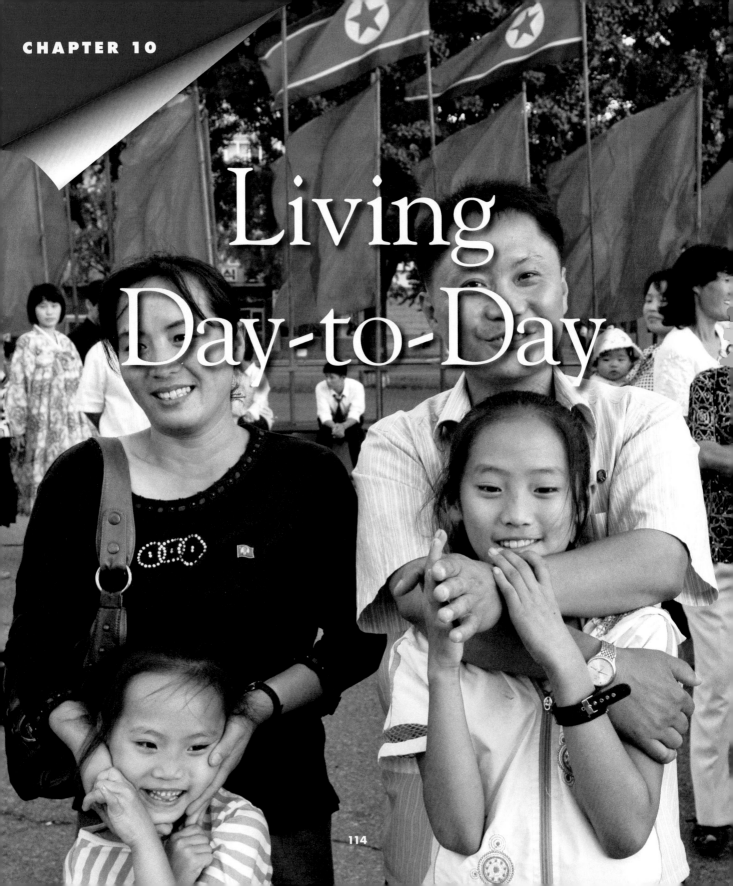

CHAPTER 10

Living Day-to-Day

AVERAGE NORTH KOREANS HAVE VERY LITTLE SAY over their day-to-day lives. They work at jobs, assigned to them by the government, six days a week. Most of their leisure time is reserved for Sunday, their day off. Most North Koreans do not earn enough to afford to attend a theater or a sporting event. Instead, they are more likely to spend their time off with family. For instance, on Sundays in Pyongyang, many people flock to Mansu Hill, where they can picnic, play music, and dance and sing.

Opposite: **A North Korean family in Pyongyang enjoys a celebration in honor of the founding of North Korea.**

Family Life and Manners

North Koreans tend not to display much emotion, even to close family members. Two boys or two girls might walk hand in hand, but generally men and women, even married couples, do not express affection in public. People are expected to show respect to their elders, and women are supposed to defer to men, whether they are their fathers, husbands, or sons.

Valuing Marriage

In Korean culture, marriage plays a very important role. To be considered a true adult, a person must have a spouse and children. As a result, very few North Koreans remain single. For instance, one survey conducted in 2008 found that only 4 percent of North Korean women between the ages of thirty and thirty-four had never been married.

The social importance of marriage was made clear in July 2012. That is when North Korean television news identified a young women, Ri Sol-ju, as Kim Jong-eun's wife. She had been attending events with the new ruler. The public appearances of the first couple marked a distinct departure from the way Kim's father, Kim Jong Il, had conducted his personal life. Kim Jong Il was never seen with his wife. By drawing attention to his wife, the boyish-looking Kim communicated to his people that he was a stable, serious adult ready to take on his new leadership role.

Any type of confrontation or displays of temper are considered inappropriate. Even looking someone directly in the eye is thought to be rude. Instead, well-mannered people are quiet and polite.

Housing and Travel

Most North Koreans live in modest homes. In the countryside, families generally have small brick houses with tile roofs. In cities, they usually live in apartments. Average workers might be assigned one-room apartments with a tiny kitchen, while officials in the military or government might live in freestanding houses with many rooms.

In both the country and the city, houses are often cold because of a lack of heating fuel. Electricity shortages also limit the use of electronics and appliances. Especially in rural areas, there is rarely enough electricity to keep the lights on after dark.

Gasoline is also in short supply. Only the elite can afford to travel by car, and their vehicles are usually old and in bad repair. Pyongyang has a large subway system, but elsewhere most people travel on foot or by bicycle.

Men bicycle in Nampo, in southwestern North Korea. Less than 1 percent of North Koreans own a car.

Food

Most North Koreans rely on meager food rations from the government, although some are able to supplement meals by buying fresh meat and produce at private markets. In rural areas, people also gather wild roots, grasses, and nuts to add to their diet. Food rations might include one or two meals of rice a day. A few times a year, for instance on the birthday of Kim Il-sung, rations include a portion of meat.

Rice has long been the staple of the Korean diet. Although Koreans use metal chopsticks as utensils, they usually eat rice with a spoon. Traditional meals combine rice with bite-size

Kindergartners eat a meal of soup and vegetables.

Kimchi

Kimchi is a popular condiment throughout the Korean Peninsula. Made of cabbage and spices, it is used to add flavor to many dishes. When preparing traditional kimchi, the cabbage is allowed to ferment, a process that takes time. This modern interpretation on kimchi, however, takes only a few minutes to put together. Have an adult help you.

Ingredients

1 tablespoon sesame oil

1 tablespoon grated ginger

2 tablespoons white vinegar

½ teaspoon each sugar, salt, and red pepper

¼ cup water

1 head napa cabbage, with the core
    removed and leaves cut into small pieces

2 cloves garlic, minced

2 green onions (scallions), sliced

Directions

1. In a bowl, mix together the oil, ginger, vinegar, sugar, salt, and red pepper.

2. Put the cabbage, garlic, and water in a saucepan, and bring the water to a boil. Reduce the heat to low, and allow the cabbage mixture to simmer for five minutes.

3. Let the cabbage cool, and add it to the sauce mixture in the bowl. Add the sliced onions and mix well.

pieces of meat or fish and some type of soup. However, the food most associated with the Korean Peninsula is kimchi—spicy pickled cabbage flavored with red pepper, ginger, and garlic. Another famous Korean dish is *bulgogi*, which is sometimes called Korean barbeque. Bulgogi is made by marinating strips of beef in soy sauce, garlic, and spices and cooking them over a charcoal or gas grill.

Most restaurants in North Korea are located in Pyongyang. Their customers are primarily elite officials. These restaurants generally serve Korean food, although a few offer Japanese, Chinese, or European cuisine.

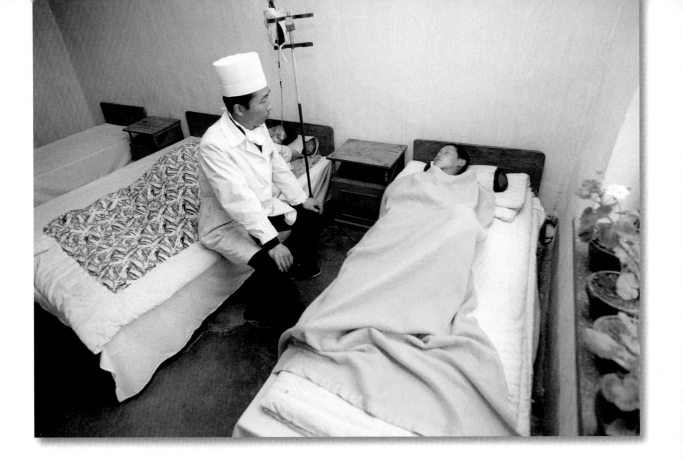

Health Care, Education, and Media

North Korea provides free health care to all its citizens. However, powerful people in the military and government have much better access to doctors and hospitals. There are not enough hospitals for the population, and the hospitals that do exist are not well funded. Many lack X-ray machines and other basic equipment.

A North Korean doctor checks on patients. On average, North Koreans live to age sixty-nine.

Jegichagi

Similar to hacky sack, *jegichagi* is a traditional Korean children's game. It is played with a jegi, an object made from a coin and paper or cloth. These materials are shaped into something that looks like a badminton birdie.

In one version of the game, each player takes a turn using his or her foot to kick the jegi into the air over and over. The winning player is the one who kicks the jegi the highest number of times before it hits the ground.

The government also oversees the country's educational system. All children are required to attend eleven years of school. Some go on to one of the more than three hundred colleges and universities in North Korea. The most prestigious is Kim Il-sung University, where students can take classes in a wide variety of fields, including physics, chemistry, atomic energy, history, politics, and the Korean language.

Most North Korean households have access to radios and television sets. However, what they can listen to or watch is limited. Like so many aspects of life in North Korea, all media—including newspapers, magazines, and television and radio shows—are under tight government control.

North Korean children receive a strong basic education. More than 99 percent of North Koreans learn to read and write.

The Korean Central Broadcasting Station in Pyongyang is responsible for broadcasts in the country. Most broadcasts are filled with flattering reports about North Korea's leaders. News in North Korea rarely mentions the troubles the nation faces, including its ailing economy and food shortages.

The North Korean government also severely limits its citizens' access to the Internet. In 2005, the country developed its own intranet, or private computer network. On the intranet, students at selected university and research institutions can gain access to some Web pages, but any sites they can look at have to be approved first by the government. More recently, a very small number of high-ranking officials and star students have been given clearance to access the actual Internet. But the majority of North Koreans have never surfed the Web.

Students work in a computer lab at Kim Il-sung University in Pyongyang. It is the nation's top university.

A man in Pyongyang talks on a cell phone. An estimated one million North Koreans have a cell-phone subscription.

News from the Outside World

Despite the government's efforts to isolate North Korea, information from the outside world is increasingly penetrating its borders. One important change is a new brisk business in cell phones smuggled in from China. North Korea bans the use of cell phones that can reach beyond its borders by anyone but high-ranking officials. But many citizens are risking harsh punishments to buy illegal Chinese prepaid phones. When North and South Korea were separated in 1945, many families lost contact with relatives on the other side of the border. Smuggled cell phones, therefore, give North Koreans a chance to finally track down and talk with long-lost family members. In these conversations, North Koreans often learn about how prosperous South Korea actually is—news that makes them begin to look at their own country in a new light.

DVDs sold illegally in towns and cities along North Korea's border with China are another important influence on the nation. The DVDs are mostly recordings of South Korean movies and television shows. Especially popular are South Korean soap operas. North Koreans are interested in these shows less for their story lines than for the window they provide into how South Koreans live. Watching the DVDs, North Korean viewers are stunned by images of well-furnished houses and stores filled with every type of food and consumer goods.

These images of South Korea provide a contrast to the harshness of life in North Korea. There also is evidence that the North Korean government is lying when it tells its citizens that South Korea is a horrible place where everyone is starving.

The Grand People's Study House, a library and educational center in Pyongyang, provides some music and videos to the public. Here, a soldier watches a video of an opera.

Another story the North Korean government tells its citizens is that South Korea desperately wants to be reunited with North Korea under the leadership of the Kim rulers. In fact, the unification of Korea is more a North Korean dream than a South Korean one. As a fairly wealthy nation, South Korea generally views unification with little enthusiasm. Despite its shared heritage with North Korea, the country is hesitant to shoulder the burden or cost of bringing its impoverished neighbor into the modern world.

Whether from relatives or television, news from the outside world serves to fuel North Koreans' already growing skepticism about their government. As Kim Jong-eun took

Children parade through the streets of Wonsan on Labor Day.

North Korean National Holidays

New Year's Day	January 1
Kim Jong Il's Birthday	February 16
Day of the Sun (celebrates Kim Il-sung's birthday)	April 15
Armed Forces Day	April 25
Labor Day	May 1
Fatherland Liberation War Victory Day	July 27
Liberation Day	August 15
Democratic People's Republic of Korea Founding Day	September 9
Korean Workers' Party Founding Day	October 10
Constitution Day	December 27

control of North Korea, he promised his people that they would soon enjoy a new prosperity. But in the first years of his rule, North Koreans saw little evidence of an improved standard of living. Rice prices shot up, and fuel and electricity remained in short supply. Reports emerged of people's frustration with the country's political system. That system, they complained, made privileged officials rich through bribes and deals with Chinese businessmen but left many North Koreans despairing and hungry.

Like his father, Kim Jong-eun told his people that they would live in a "strong and prosperous nation" by 2012, the one-hundredth anniversary of his grandfather's birth. But for most North Korean people, that promise has not yet been fulfilled. The future of North Korea is hard to predict. But as North Koreans learn more about the outside world, they may become less patient with their current leadership and begin to imagine a new and different path forward for their country.

Timeline

NORTH KOREAN HISTORY

The Old Choson civilization emerges along the Taedong River.	ca. 300s BCE
The Korean Peninsula is unified under the rule of the Silla kingdom.	668 CE
The Choson dynasty establishes control over Korea.	1392
Korea repels a series of Japanese invasions.	1590s

WORLD HISTORY

ca. 2500 BCE	The Egyptians build the pyramids and the Sphinx in Giza.
ca. 563 BCE	The Buddha is born in India.
313 CE	The Roman emperor Constantine legalizes Christianity.
610	The Prophet Muhammad begins preaching a new religion called Islam.
1054	The Eastern (Orthodox) and Western (Roman Catholic) Churches break apart.
1095	The Crusades begin.
1215	King John seals the Magna Carta.
1300s	The Renaissance begins in Italy.
1347	The plague sweeps through Europe.
1453	Ottoman Turks capture Constantinople, conquering the Byzantine Empire.
1492	Columbus arrives in North America.
1500s	Reformers break away from the Catholic Church, and Protestantism is born.
1776	The U.S. Declaration of Independence is signed.
1789	The French Revolution begins.
1865	The American Civil War ends.
1879	The first practical lightbulb is invented.

NORTH KOREAN HISTORY

Korea becomes a colony of Japan.	**1910**
World War II ends with the northern half of Korea occupied by troops from the Soviet Union.	**1945**
The Democratic People's Republic of Korea (North Korea) is established.	**1948**
North Korea invades South Korea, beginning the Korean War.	**1950**
An armistice ends the fighting in the Korean War.	**1953**
North Korea loses economic aid when the Soviet Union collapses.	**1991**
A famine kills as many as three million North Koreans.	**mid-1990s**
North Korean leader Kim Il-sung dies.	**1994**
Kim Jong Il succeeds his father as ruler of North Korea.	**1997**
The leaders of North and South Korea meet for the first time at a summit in Pyongyang.	**2000**
North Korea admits that it has been developing a secret nuclear weapons program.	**2002**
Tensions grow between North and South Korea after the sinking of the South Korean warship *Cheonan*.	**2010**
Kim Jong Il dies; his son Kim Jong-eun is named his successor.	**2011**
North Korea holds a lavish celebration of the one-hundredth anniversary of the birth of Kim Il-sung.	**2012**

WORLD HISTORY

1914	World War I begins.
1917	The Bolshevik Revolution brings communism to Russia.
1929	A worldwide economic depression begins.
1939	World War II begins.
1945	World War II ends.
1969	Humans land on the Moon.
1975	The Vietnam War ends.
1989	The Berlin Wall is torn down as communism crumbles in Eastern Europe.
1991	The Soviet Union breaks into separate states.
2001	Terrorists attack the World Trade Center in New York City and the Pentagon near Washington, D.C.
2004	A tsunami in the Indian Ocean destroys coastlines in Africa, India, and Southeast Asia.
2008	The United States elects its first African American president.

Fast Facts

Official name: The Democratic People's Republic of Korea

Capital: Pyongyang

Official language: Korean

Nampo

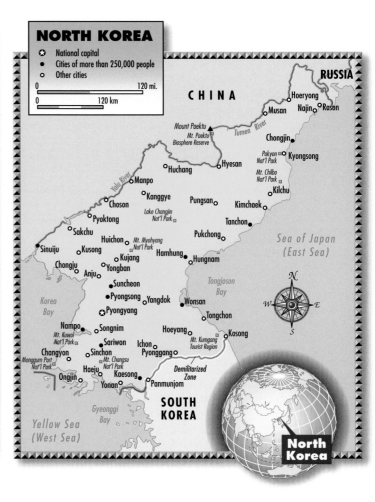

North Korean flag

Official religion:	None
Year of founding:	1948
National anthem:	"Aegukka" ("The Patriotic Song")
Government:	Communist dictatorship
Head of state:	President of the Presidium of the Supreme People's Assembly
Head of government:	Premier
Area of country:	47,399 square miles (122,763 sq km)
Latitude and longitude of geographic center:	40°N, 127°E
Bordering countries:	China to the north, Russia to the northeast, and South Korea to the south
Highest elevation:	Mount Paektu, 9,003 feet (2,744 m) above sea level
Lowest elevation:	Sea of Japan, sea level
Average daily high temperature:	83°F (28°C) in August; 29°F (−2°C) in January
Average annual rainfall:	9.9 inches (25.1 cm) in July; 0.5 inches (1.3 cm) in February

Mount Kumgang

Tower of the Juche Idea

National population (2011 est.):	24.4 million	
Population of major cities (2008 est.):	Pyongyang	3,255,300
	Hamhung	768,600
	Chongjin	667,900
	Nampo	366,800
	Wonsan	363,127

Landmarks:
- ▶ *Complex of Koguryo Tombs*, Pyongyang
- ▶ *Mansudae Grand Monument*, Pyongyang
- ▶ *Mount Paektu*, Ryanggang Province
- ▶ *Tower of the Juche Idea*, Pyongyang

Economy: In North Korea, all trade and industry are controlled by the state. Its government-operated collective farms produce potatoes, corn, soybeans, wheat, tobacco, and cotton, as well as animal products, such as eggs, beef, goat meat, and milk. Industrial goods made in North Korea include machines, textiles, and weapons. The government has trouble feeding its people and relies on financial and food aid from international organizations and political allies, especially China. In recent years, the government has experimented with some modest economic reforms, but North Korea's economy continues to falter.

Currency

Currency: The North Korean won. In March 2013, US$1.00 equaled 132 won, and 1 won equaled 0.89 cents

System of weights and measures: Metric system

Literacy rate (2011): 99%

Schoolchildren

An Kum Ae

Common Korean words and phrases:

Ne	Yes
Aniyo	No
Annyong haseyo	Hello/How are you?
Annyonghi kyeseyo	Good-bye
Shille hamnida	Excuse me
Komapsumnida	Thank you
Ch'on manyeo	You're welcome
Chuseyo	Please
Ch'oesong hamnida	Sorry

Prominent North Koreans:

An Kum Ae   (1980–)
Olympic gold medal-winning judo athlete

Ch'oe Che-u   (1824–1864)
Founder of the Ch'ondogyo religion

Hong Sok-chung   (1941–)
Novelist

Kim Il-sung   (1912–1994)
Former North Korean ruler

Kim Jong-eun   (ca. 1983–)
North Korean ruler

Kim Jong Il   (1941–2011)
Former North Korean ruler

Sun Myung Moon   (1920–2012)
Founder of the Unification Church

To Find Out More

Books

▶ Hart, Joyce. *Kim Jong Il: Leader of North Korea.* New York: Rosen, 2008.

▶ Salter, Christopher L. *North Korea.* New York: Chelsea House Publishing, 2007.

▶ Senker, Cath. *North Korea and South Korea.* New York: Rosen, 2013.

DVDs

▶ *A State of Mind.* Directed by Daniel Gordon. New York: Kino International, 2006.

▶ *Inside North Korea.* Directed by Peter Yost. Washington, DC: National Geographic Video, 2007.

▶ Visit this Scholastic Web site for more information on North Korea:
www.factsfornow.scholastic.com
Enter the keywords **North Korea**

Index

Page numbers in *italics* indicate illustrations.

Korean Workers' Party (KWP), 47, 52, 60, 61, 62, 65, 66
Koryo dynasty, 38, 39
labor camps, 48, 54, 62, 63, 84, 86
language and, 89
legislative branch, 59, 60–61
literature and, 103–104, *103*
loyalty badges, 101–102
ministers, 59
Ministry of Public Security, 63
Mongol Empire, 38–39
National Defense Commission, 52, 61
People's Armed Forces, 59
performing arts and, 104, 105
premiers, 59, 60–61
Presidium, 59
prison camps, 54, *62*, 63, 84, 97, 108
propaganda, 10, 48–49, 50, 86–87, 102, 123, 125–126
provincial governments, 66
Qing dynasty, 40
religion and, 91, 98–99
secrecy of, 10, 16–17, 48, 49, 63, *63*, 65
social classes and, 84
songun policy, 15, *51*, 69, 77
Soviet Union and, 43, 44, 45, 47, 50
Sunshine Policy, 55
Supreme People's Assembly (SPA), 59, 60, 62
Three Kingdoms period, 36–37, *36*
United States and, 43
vice premiers, 59
Grand People's Study House, 104, *125*
guerrilla war, 42, 45, 106
guest worker program, 80, 81
gymnastics, 112

H
Hamhung, 25, *25*, 49, 83
Hangul writing system, 89, *89*
Han rulers, 35

health care, 47, 121, *121*
Heaven Lake, 20, 27, *27*
historical maps. *See also* maps.
    Choson Dynasty, 1392–1910, *40*
    Korean War, 1950–1953, *45*
    The Three Kingdoms and Unified Silla, *36*
hockey, 110
holidays, 9, 10, *126*, 127
Hong Sok-chung, 104, 133
housing, *24*, 69, 84, 87, 116–117
Hwang Jin-i (Hong Sok-chung), 104, *104*

I
immigration, 83
imports, 77, 80
International Friendship Exhibition, 102, *102*
Internet, 63, 123
intranet, 123
iron industry, 25
islands, 21

J
Japan, 38, 40, 41–42, *43*, 54, 88, 97, 105, 106
Japanese language, 89
jegichagi (game), 121
jobs, 49, 72, 73–74, 75, 77, 80–81, *80*, 84, 85, 103, 115
Jong Il Peak, 23, *23*
journalism, 11, 16, 65, *65*, 85–86
judicial branch of government, 61, 62–63
Jungjong, king of Choson dynasty, 104

K
Kaesong, 38, *39*, 66, *73*, 92
Kaesong Industrial Region, 78–79
kimchi (food), 119, *119*, 120
Kim Il-sung. *See also* government.
    art and, *12*, 48, *48*, 67, 101, 102
    birthday celebration, 9, 10–11, *12*, *14*, *15*, 118
    criticism of, 48

death of, 50, 56, 67
education and, 47
gifts presented to, 102
health care and, 47
International Friendship Exhibition and, 102
kimilsungia orchid, 32
Kim Jong-eun and, 55
Korean War and, 45, 47, *47*
Korean Workers' Party (KWP) and, 47
literature and, 103–104, *103*
loyalty badges and, 101–102
military and, 47–48
mother of, 95
as premier, 16, 44–45, *44*, 50, 52, 61, 133
propaganda and, 48–49, 50
Soviet Union and, *44*, 47, 50
Kim Il-sung Square, 9, 13, *15*
Kim Il-sung Stadium, 110
Kim Il-sung University, 67, 99, 122, *123*
Kim Jong-eun. *See also* government.
    art and, 101
    Kim Il-sung and, 55
    Kim Jong Il and, 56, *56*
    marriage of, 116, *116*
    military and, *14*, 15, *57*, 59, 61, 68
    nuclear program and, 56–57
    physical description of, 55
    as premier, 10, *10*, 13, 55–57, *57*, *58*, 61, 127, 133
    propaganda and, 48
    speeches of, 14–16, *14*
    sports and, 112
Kim Jong Il. *See also* government.
    art and, 11, 12, *12*, 101, 102
    birth of, 23
    death of, 10, 23, 56, *56*
    film industry and, 106–107, 108
    flooding and, 53
    Kim Jong-eun and, 56, *56*

Meet the Author

A GRADUATE OF SWARTHMORE COLLEGE, LIZ Sonneborn is a full-time writer living in Brooklyn, New York. She has written more than ninety nonfiction books for children, young adults, and adults on a wide variety of subjects. Her books include *The American West: An Illustrated History, Ancient China, The Vietnamese Americans, Chronology of American Indian History, Harriet Beecher Stowe,* and *The Great Irish Famine.*

Sonneborn has written numerous books in the Enchantment of the World series, including *Yemen, Pakistan, Iraq,* and *The United Arab Emirates. North Korea,* however, presented a unique research challenge. Because the government places such tight controls on information about its people and society, it was difficult to get a handle on what life in North Korea is really like. Scholarly experts on North Korea can only speculate on what is going on in the government. As a result, Sonneborn had to be careful to qualify their findings, making clear in the text that certain conclusions were only the best guesses of knowledgeable people rather than hard facts. To get a sense of everyday life in North Korea, she sought out accounts of North Koreans who had escaped their country in recent years.

But she had to approach even their stories with some skepticism. Because so few people actually have succeeded in fleeing North Korea, their views, impressions, and experiences might not always represent those of the average citizen of their country.

Not only was it tricky to weigh the accuracy of reports on and from North Korea. It was also a challenge to keep the focus on the North Koreans themselves. "In researching North Korea," Sonneborn explains, "I realized how much reportage on North Korea in the United States is about one of two things: the peculiar behavior and appearance of Kim

Jong Il and Kim Jong-eun or the government's constant stream of threats to its perceived enemies. Between comedians joking about the Kim leaders and reporters stoking fear of North Korea in the media, it is easy for people to view not just its government, but its people, as both ridiculous and terrifying. I wanted to resist that temptation in his book. Based on the limited information we have on North Korean life, I tried to present North Koreans fairly. Rather than depicting them as inherently silly or evil, I wanted to show them as a beleaguered people who struggle to survive great hardship every day while living under a dishonest and repressive regime."

Photo Credits